10

JESUS

CHRISTIANS WITHOUT JESUS IN HELL

A CHRISTIAN BOOK

Luis Dávila

100% JESUS. CHRISTIANS WITHOUT JESUS IN HELL

A CHRISTIAN BOOK by Luis Dávila

ISBN: 9781098818166

Sello: Independently published

Copyright © 2018 by Luis Dávila

Originally published in Spanish under the title:
Cristianos en el infierno. Independently published
(April 18, 2017)

Translated by Rudiany Buzcete

Copyright © 2018 by Luis Dávila

Content

Preamble
Valencia, Venezuela

The interviewee, a woman of God to whom Jesus Christ guided me, concluded by saying:

—The greatest deception of Satan within the churches comes from the preaching of grace without mentioning the necessity of repentance.

Satan? Fooling ourselves inside the church? At first it was hard for me to admit it but it's a reality.

Those who don't know me, I tell you. In 2013 I gave my life to Jesus Christ after surviving a traffic accident. From the impact, despite my drunkenness, I remember a terrifying emptiness just before I thought: I'm safe, thank God I'm still alive. Although I wasn't looking for God, in His love and mercy He sought me out, He first loved me, and then Jesus Christ called me to His service.

I live the circumstances according to God's plan for me; I study the bible to understand its purposes. Between dreams, revelations and his word, Jesus Christ teaches or warns me. In dreams I saw something of the Heaven; and I've felt Hell twice, it's real, and there are Christians suffering there. Before writing this book, God led me to read the testimony of a woman in the outer darkness and the lake of fire, two biblical places.

I must insist hell is real. After two books, one night, in the solitude of my apartment, I asked God: Father, teach me something more of the suffering of hell, I need to write with arguments.

That same night, suddenly, I felt again that frightening emptiness of the accident. This time it was not an instant but several seconds, the experience was abysmal, I thought about committing suicide, I even started walking towards the balcony to throw myself, when, just before opening the door, God returned to my spirit.

That is the best way to explain it. God took his spirit away from me and I felt absolutely alone. Human beings, believe, or not, in God, we have our spirit connected to the creator; When we die, if we go to hell, the first suffering is that terrifying void; something inexplicable that I never want to feel again. Do you want to know more about hell? God asked in my heart.

No, beloved Father — I answered still anguished.

Given my task as a writer, the Chief, Jesus Christ, configured, in his own way, my meeting with a friend and ex—partner from work. Upon hearing my testimony, he recalled an industrial accident where he almost lost his life. Surprised, he told me:

—I didn't see hell; I only experienced part of the suffering. I felt despair, that day I checked, it's real.

Among other details, that friend told me his desperation to crave a drop of water in his mouth. Immediately, I remembered the Gospel of Luke where Jesus taught about the man who died and his soul went to hell, there he cried out for mercy, he suffered, he asked for at least a drop of water on his tongue because he was burning in flames.

From my friend, I heard more of suffering in hell. God taught me through the experience of another. However, months later, Jesus led me to read the testimony of a servant of God who traveled for thirty to hell. Among so many available testimonies, I received the address of the Holy Spirit to believe that. In the outer darkness and the lake of fire, Jesus explained to him why those souls are there. She saw Christians, I share these two cases:

In the first, spears pierced the heart of someone, who suffered, and felt it. Jesus explained to him: that man was a preacher of the word of God preached the truth and led many to salvation; then Satan deceived him, the preacher let evil enters his heart. Little by little, he began to preach half lies and half truth. Jesus tried to correct him, but he kept teaching doctrines out of those revealed in the Bible, he said that God didn't send anyone to hell because God was good to do that; He taught that one could sin and still go to heaven without repenting. In his love Jesus called him, he looked for him, but, that man didn't want to repent, Satan deceived him and he deceived many more.

In the second case, the servant of God visited the outer darkness, a place mentioned in the Bible, a part of hell. There, Jesus Christ showed him children of the kingdom of God, Christians who turned away from Him after beginning to follow Him. Servants who chose the pleasures above the will of God; Christians who love the world above Jesus; people who turned away from Him to enjoy sin; believers who could not stand the truth and holiness. It's better not to have begun to follow Jesus than to turn away from Him after following Him and serving Him. The warning of that servant of God is also in my heart, if we repent of sins Jesus is faithful to cleanse us from evil. He is the defense lawyer, but we need to repent because, if we don't, we will be thrown into hell, into outer darkness. Believe this warning.

Dear reader, this book was written as a warning for compassion to millions of believers in Jesus Christ who are deceived by Satan through the preaching of grace without the need of repentance. In my case, despite trying to lead a pleasant lifestyle before God, daily the Holy Spirit convicts me and guides me to repent of my sins, although sometimes they seem insignificant. In several dreams, Jesus Christ has warned me, I can end up in hell for at least two reasons: for not fulfilling my purpose for Him and / or for not repenting in time of sins. Until the last breath Satan yearns for our soul. We must take care of our salvation, we can lose it.

Introduction

God loves us, Jesus loves us and Holy Spirit also loves us, the love of the three of them is perfect. As Christians, we enjoy their inexhaustible love, they protect us, and they want the best for us.

The first one, God takes care of us as a responsible father; he respects the free will of his children, protects us and warns us to protect us from the evil one. Jesus Christ takes care of us, warns us like our elder brother, and, Holy Spirit, our faithful friend, and reminds us of his warnings in the spirit. That is, as Christians, children of God, we have all three loving us and protecting us from the evil one, above all, warning us not to be deceived.

I emphasize "warn" because this book was written as a yellow traffic sign indicating "caution". My intention is never to judge anyone; who makes traffic signals is not happy to see accidents happen to ignore it. On the contrary, is happy to know the number of lives saved by being cautious before the existing danger.

Among several books on the agenda, the Chief, Jesus Christ, changed my plans suddenly. The preaching of grace without repentance is a spiritual cancer. God will destroy Satan's deceived, give us the necessary revelation, we can lose salvation.

God gave us a will of our own, free will. We can choose between serving Jesus Christ or Satan. The planet works under the influence of good or evil, there is no middle ground, nobody is neutral. Every person on earth is in favor of or against God.

As we know, the war between good and evil is based on the rebellion of Lucifer, Satan, who was expelled from heaven. Hell wasn't made for the human being, that place of suffering was created by God for Satan and his rebellious angels, and we must understand it. The Heavenly Father doesn't want any human being to spend eternity there, much less his children, the heirs of the kingdom, who have the privilege of being children through Jesus Christ.

That is why Jesus warned us. Let's read the Gospel according to Matthew where He explained clearly that children of the kingdom can be cast into outer darkness; where there crying and gnashing of teeth.

In several dreams I was warned about losing my salvation. In one I saw myself at a party. While there someone asked me: why don't you have adequate clothes? Surprised I yelled at my best friend: why didn't you bring my clothes? Before answering I was thrown out of the place, I fell into a kind of river of darkness and, just as I was going to the bottom of the abyss, I grabbed something. There, I woke up in anguish.

Lord Jesus, was this a dream of yours? — I said even with my heart racing, the feeling of being thrown out was terrifying.

Since not all dreams come from God, I prefer to ask him before looking for the revelation.

Yes — Jesus answered in my heart.

Immediately, I remembered a case of the Gospel of Matthew where something similar happened. I paraphrase it for you: A king came to receive the guests but saw that a man was not dressed for the wedding, when asking: how are you here without wedding clothes? The man had no answer, and then the king sent to throw him into the darkness outside.

That morning, I thought about that dream several times, I looked for answers; I needed to know what was I doing wrong? Without finding any obvious sin in my conscience, before my constant memories of the abyss, suddenly, God responded to my heart:

—If you let grow that root of disbelief that will be your eternal destiny.

To my surprise, the trial against me didn't come because of the sin of the commonly known; the problem was in a doubt in my heart, God had made me a promise, it depended on my purpose for Jesus Christ, and I was hesitating. God promised to reconcile me with my wife, as it took to happen I began to doubt. Without reconciliation I couldn't fulfill the purpose of Jesus Christ in my life. If the incredulity grew I could stop believing and if I stopped believing I couldn't fulfill the purpose. As a result, I could lose my salvation.

We are used to associate the word sin with stealing, killing, adulterating, among others. That is one of Satan's deceptions because sin is any disobedience to the will of God. When God commands us to do A, if we do B, we are in sin. If Jesus Christ calls us to fulfill a task for Him, our only option is to do it, on the contrary, we are in rebellion.

The worst mistake of a Christian, man or woman, is to receive God's direction to do something and not do it. We can have a call to serve in A and we prefer to serve in B, be A and B anything. When we know the will of God and don't fulfill it as He wants, we are in rebellion. God always has a plan. If Jesus needs us in A, it's in A, not in B. If we do something for God, but He commanded us to do something else, we are in rebellion to put our will on His.

It's indispensable to understand, God is the General of good in this spiritual war on planet earth. Let's make an analogy with the army. If we were chosen by Him for the navy, it's for the navy, not for aviation; yes, today, the Chief, Jesus, ordered us to use a pistol, and we shouldn't use a sword. Every man or woman, believer, obedient to Jesus, must fight against his own will. To replace the will of Jesus Christ with ours, under the "I think is better", is something serious. That opens doors of rebellion, without realizing we move away from the will of God, and without suspecting it we can be obeying the devil.

In the psalms we are warned to be careful with the little foxes that can destroy the vineyard. Satan is cunning, even if it sounds exaggerated, he can start deceiving us with, for example, God sent you to eat banana, but better eat pineapple. Without knowing it, you were allergic to pineapple, you ate it, and you almost died. Because of that, God sent you to eat banana.

In my case, after that warning dream I needed to repent and ask God for forgiveness for feeding that root of disbelief in my life.

The problem was not the disbelief that Satan tried to sow, the serious thing was letting it grow even knowing the will of God. Without suspecting it, in my heart, a root of incredulity was growing. When he stopped believing, disobeying Jesus was easier.

The grace to forgive me has been present, in my Christian life, when I repent. If I make a mistake, I appeal to God's forgiveness through his grace, but I need to repent not only from my lips, but in my heart, that is, in a sincere way. I must not abuse the grace, I need to repent. Lack of repentance can lead to pride.

If we go to heaven we receive a glorified spiritual body for our enjoyment, if we go to hell the soul suffers, the five senses remain. Twenty years ago, I checked the spiritual body. One night I left my body; first, I saw myself in bed sleeping, then I walked through the apartment, I heard my father snoring and I went back into my earthly body.

At the time, I didn't know, but, my experience is consistent with the testimony of the servant of God, she assures him, when dying the five senses remain, I believe him, I checked that night. In hell the soul maintains the senses, you really suffer.

With the revelation of eternity we believe in the possible destinies after death, well-being or suffering, both eternal, and depend on us. If we are saved, we must take care of our salvation.

As Christians we know the obvious cases, people destined for eternal suffering. The Apostle Paul in his letter to the Corinthian church explained it: people who indulge in sexual sin or worship idols or commit adultery or are prostitutes or practice homosexuality or are thieves or greedy or drunk or insult or swindle people. Although those cases are obvious, they are not the only ones.

Any Christian can lose their salvation. The main deception of Satan within the church is in generating self-confidence in the people of Jesus Christ, to guide us to make his own plans above the will of God, making us believe that grace replaces obedience. Many deceived believe, God loves me and that's why I can disobey him.

Beloved brother or sister in Christ, the day when we receive Jesus in our hearts we become children of God. Every son or daughter must obey his father; we need to obey God in everything, until the last breath here on earth.

If my son violates earthly laws, he goes to jail. I can be sad but he suffers the sentence. The laws are the same for everyone; if he violates them, he condemns himself; he is not condemned by the one who wrote the law. Similarly, it happens in the spiritual world, the only difference is that God, the Creator of the law, is our Heavenly Father, but He is also Just Judge. I insist, without repentance there is no forgiveness of sins.

The blood of Jesus Christ cleanses us but repentance is necessary. Certainly, the Bible mentions as the only sin that cannot be forgiven for blasphemy against the Holy Spirit, any other sin can be forgiven, as long as we repent with a sincere heart, in other words, genuinely.

The Heavenly Father through repentance doesn't give us what we deserve (punishment); and by his grace we receive what we don't deserve (forgiveness). As Christians we need to understand the grace-repentance balance to protect salvation. We must seek greater spiritual maturity until we know Jesus; obey Jesus by love, beyond obeying him only out of fear or convenience.

This book, it's a timely warning before the spiritual warfare in which we are immersed. Pastors, leaders, all the people of God must be ready; the enemy is cunning and is deceiving inside churches, where a balanced gospel is not being preached. In hell there are Christians because they were deceived, shepherds, sheep, both.

Spiritual warfare within churches

If we understand the existence of the invisible world that dominates the visible, we understand how human beings make decisions under the influence of good or evil. In this book I will use the term "angels" to refer to God's allies and "demons" for the devil's henchmen.

To date, in my personal experience I haven't seen angels or demons, but I feel his presence in places, people and even in things. The invisible influence on all our visible life is amazing.

From the story of the servant of God in hell, and from the Bible, I know that our struggle is not against flesh or blood, it's not against human beings; the war as the Apostle Paul explained to the Ephesians is against evil rulers and authorities of the invisible world, powerful forces of this dark world, evil spirits of heavenly places. That's the Heaven we see, the place where we live.

In hell, she saw how Satan directed great demons that sent little ones to break homes, destroy families, deceive and even seduce weak Christians. The devil told them that strong Christians had the power to expel them. According to our spiritual strength, we fight with great or small demons, until we can have demons assigned personally and familiarly.

16

Once sent to earth, the demons do their homework, without us seeing them, nor suspecting them.

In relation to believers who ended up in hell to get away from God I remember that the servant saw suffering a woman who died of cancer. Although that woman knew Jesus, she attributed her illness to God, never repented and didn't believe in the gospel. When she was a child Jesus Christ called her to serve him, she delayed fulfilling her purpose by saying "I will serve you later". That moment didn't come, and when she died it was too late. She thought that Jesus would wait for her all her life and it didn't happen that way.

In my personal experience, I understood it recently; God sought me from childhood, without my knowing it. Then he returned to look for me as a teenager, then I began to walk with Jesus through a Christian friend, but when she rejected me, the devil deceived me, guiding me to think that God had rejected me. From there, I went away some twenty years until, in his grace and mercy, for the third time, in my adulthood, Jesus Christ sought me.

Although I felt death in the accident, I didn't decide to follow Jesus Christ at that moment, I confess. God had saved me, I knew it, I was grateful but that was it. However, with his love, latter, in a dream, I saw the following warning and decided to avoid it:

In that dream I saw my wife desperate for the city placing help-seeking ads with my son's face, under the title "Wanted, Missing Child".

When I woke up crying, I asked God for explanations, in my heart, firmly, He answered:

—If you don't change your lifestyle, that will happen.

Although Jesus saved my life I continued to lead an unpleasant life before God. Upon hearing that warning I cried with anguish, in the end I said:

—I will work for you until the last day of my life, but, don't let that happen to my son.

Without God asking me, I made a pact with Him. This is what I assumed from that day. Five years have passed, and that hasn't happen. Jesus Christ fulfilled his part, now I must and I want to fulfill mine in gratitude.

I bring this case to an end to emphasize that even on the verge of death, our stubbornness can lead us to reject God's call. In his love and mercy, Jesus used my weak point, my son; I didn't care about my life, I could lose it, but I was not able to risk the life of my only son. From there, I accepted, I began to obey his call. To date, He has made me a writer and athlete for his glory. I fulfill their assignments but that never indicates that I cannot lose my salvation. The struggle between good and evil, for the eternal destiny of my soul, will only end with my last breath before dying. In a dream I saw Jesus Christ, accompanied by my father and an uncle, receiving me in heaven, that is his wish, nor my father, my uncle, nor I can trust ourselves.

Why cannot we trust?

Because, in addition to the associated biblical quotes, I also remember another of the cases of Christians, that the servant of God saw in hell.

She saw and heard a man preaching the gospel in hell. Astonished she consulted Jesus who explained that the man had been a preacher of the gospel on earth. One time he preached the truth, served God, and then didn't believe in hell; he began to preach what people wanted to hear. He raised his own rules about good and evil, led many to turn away from Jesus. That preacher, although he knew the truth, didn't genuinely repent and never returned to Jesus Christ even though God sought him, Jesus waited, but man allowed Satan to fill his heart with lies, he preferred sin, sometimes he repented, but half of that It was not enough. The word of God is true; when he died he had his destiny in hell.

Servant or servant of Jesus Christ it's my duty to warn, the gifts are irrevocable but we decided to use them for God or for the devil. Deliver me Jesus from writing books distorting the truth of the gospel or running for my boasting, because I could continue to use my gifts but in hell.

19

This book, besides being a public warning, is an exhortation for me. As I write, I receive fresh revelation, with the information the fear of the Lord takes over more and more of my whole being.

Luis, are you afraid of hell? —Commented a Christian friend, when we talked about it.

I fear God, who can destroy both the soul and the body in hell — I thought immediately.

The spiritual warfare within churches is a reality, Satan uses tricks from pulpits where the truth is preached half—heartedly, without balance, as I have already mentioned, they preach grace without repentance. But, that is not the only strategy of Satan.

The servant of God also saw in hell a woman who went to church to seduce men. The Bible states that all adulterers will have their share in the lake of fire. Although Jesus sought her to serve him she preferred to serve Satan. Adultery is serious. Christians, woman, man, we can end up in hell for that. The issue is serious, because, even without executing adultery, wishing someone out of wedlock can be considered by God as adultery in the heart.

Divorce is another serious issue in Christians. Even though I committed adultery and divorce, God sent me back to my wife. For me, any relationship was different from my wife, it's adultery. Wife with her husband, husband with his wife, another different relationship is adultery. Some Christians appeal to the Old Testament, to the letter of divorce of Moses to try to justify his divorce. Jesus explained it, which was a concession from God for the hardness of their hearts. God abhors divorce, the Bible says.

The issue of divorce is serious. He heard various justifications among my acquaintances, above all, I hear the argument of happiness, many people say:

—God made me to be happy.

I cannot find that affirmation in the Bible, at least not so overwhelming. I haven't read "please do ..." when God spoke to someone. He always gave the order; it was for the good of the person.

I don't imagine my father telling me: "please, Luis, eat" or "Luis, please, bathe." We ourselves, or our neighbor, are the beneficiaries of God's order; or those affected, if we disobey.

God wants us to be happy, it's evident, but true happiness is the result of obeying Him through Jesus and the Holy Spirit in us. Obedience brings us to intimacy with them three.

Hence, another of Satan's strategies, within the church, is to use men and women in congregations to seduce and break families.

One night, in a church, halfway through the service, I saw a lush woman walking down the main corridor with a short skirt, her body was perfect.

That time, I remembered. The servant of God saw in hell how Satan disguised demons as beautiful men and women, that exuberant lady was sent from evil, I felt it immediately.

Removing Christians from the congregations is part of all spiritual warfare within churches.

I remember how, the servant of God saw another woman in hell who in pain said to Jesus:

—Sir, I was a member of your church and it was good, you called me to serve and obey you. I did it like that.

In this regard, Jesus with love answered him:

—I looked for you, I loved you and I brought you to me, but, with your lips you said that you loved me while your heart didn't say it. I wanted to use you, but, you wanted more to the world than to me. It's true; you were a member of a church, but, gathering you does not take you to heaven. You did not forgive those who hurt you, you pretended to love me and to serve me when you were with Christians, but, far from them, you sinned, I looked for you, you didn't regret it. You enjoyed double life, you knew the truth, but, you judged your brothers in Christ and he believed you better than them while there was a great sin in you. You judged the external and they were children of God. If you had served me with sincerity you would not suffer this. You cannot serve Satan and God at the same time.

In the Bible, in the Gospel of Matthew, we can read how Jesus was firm about it, when he said:

—Not everyone who calls me "Lord, Lord!" will enter the kingdom of heaven. Only those who truly do the will of my Father who is in heaven will enter.

To ignore that theme in the church is another deception of Satan. "Lord" indicates "Lordship", that is, someone's authority over us. In my case, Jesus Christ revealed himself to me as "Chief". I report to Christ. Boss is a synonym of Lord, easier to understand, as Chief I always remember, Jesus is the boss.

However, depending on the situation, I sometimes refer to Him as my Savior, Pastor, Provider, Big Brother, recognizing Him as "Lord".

Beyond the word Lord in the mouth, it's truly doing the will of God in everything, through Jesus Christ directing our whole life. My son explained it to him in the following way: you know Messi (the soccer player), you have seen him on TV, but Messi doesn't know you. Likewise, we know about Jesus, but the important thing is that Jesus knows us. As His creation, He knows us; We need to reach intimacy with Him, obedience, make Him our Lord.

Not even exercising spiritual power, through Jesus, indicates his lordship. In this regard, He taught:

—The day of the trial, many will tell me: "Lord! We prophesied, we drove out demons in your name and we did many miracles in your name. "But He will answer them: "I never knew you. Get away from me, you, who violate the laws of God. "

As we see the warning is biblical; also the servant of God saw Christians in eternal suffering.

In another part of hell, she heard a woman:

—Jesus is the way, the truth and the life. No one can come to Christ except through him. Jesus is the light of the world. Come to Jesus, and He will save you.

Upon hearing it, the lost souls around him cursed or asked, is there hope?

Regarding that woman, Jesus told the servant:

—I call people to my service, but, if they don't want my Spirit, then I move away. She answered the call and did good things for me, led many to holiness and was faithful to her home. One day, her husband committed adultery and although he asked for forgiveness, she hardened her heart, did not want to forgive him or save her marriage. She knew it, she had to forgive him, but she never did. Her anger sowed roots, she didn't want to give Him her anger, she claimed that she was the saint and the husband the sinner. Anger with her husband became anger with others. She quoted the Bible, but, she didn't forgive her husband, in the end she killed the husband and the other woman, and then committed suicide. Satan took possession of her.

The lack of forgiveness is an issue that is not addressed within the church that is another of the deceptions of Satan in the congregations, on the Christians. In apocalypse, we can read how in the kingdom of God nothing unclean will enter, and a heart with a lack of forgiveness is considered unclean by Jesus. In fact, in his word, in Matthew, we can read the case of the debtor who did not forgive his partner.

Briefly, I remind you of that case:

For love, the king forgave the debt of a servant, but, this did not forgive the debt of his companion. Seeing that, other servants told the king, who got angry and sent his servant to prison.

At the end of that parable, Jesus taught:

—That will make my heavenly Father to you if you refuse to forgive your brothers from your heart.

Therefore, the lack of forgiveness is serious, it's a sin of the heart and Jesus Christ warned of its consequences.

In the previous cases, we approach what was seen by the Servant of God with regard to Christians; Knower's of the truth, who lost their salvation.

However, many congregations are made up of self-called "Christian" people, who consider that going to church from time to time is enough; they dismiss the need to lead a pleasant lifestyle before God. Regarding this, she saw a young man who heard the gospel and frequently attended church, but he preferred the liquor and pleasures of the world above attending his call. Jesus explained:

—That young man told me "I will live my life for you, one day, Jesus". But that day didn't come because he died in a traffic accident after a party.

Satan deceived that young man until the end, and he does it with thousands of people who think the same. Heeding the call of Jesus Christ is indispensable. Not answering, not fulfilling our call is serious. Even our family cannot be above the purpose for which God chooses us one day.

The church is the body of Jesus Christ and spiritual warfare is evident, even, within it.

Our pride sometimes prevents us from admitting mistakes and asking for forgiveness. When we know that we are children of God it's easy to seek Jesus in solitude and repent, humble ourselves before Him; but sometimes we create arguments to think that we are right. From Adam, we are easily deceived.

A valid tool against Satan's deceptions is repentance. The enemy is cunning; we need to read the Bible, because Jesus Christ taught:

—If you love your father or your mother more than me, you are not worthy to be mine; If you love your son or your daughter more than me, you are not worthy to be mine. If you refuse to take your cross and follow me, you are not worthy to be mine. If you cling to your life, you will lose it; but, if you give your life for me, you will save it.

Those words are hard, but, appropriate. It was hard for me to understand them. I learned how, for the sake of my family, I need to love God above them. Following Jesus Christ involves taking a spiritual cross, the purpose for which we are called, following it.

Several years passed before I discovered my idolatry for my son. My love was not pure, there was an emotional bond wrong. If I was with my son I was happy, if my son wasn't with me I was unhappy. Then, if my son called me I was happy, if he did not call then I would stay sad. It's my example with my son, but, it can happen with other relatives or people.

I knew love when I recognized the love of God. Now I love Jesus over my son, so I managed to love my son more and better. Likewise, I learned to love my parents, brothers, wife, and neighbor. I receive love; I am filled with God, to love everyone.

God is the inexhaustible source of love, He is love.

Obeying God means carrying a cross; Jesus did it and we will too. In his case, the cross was visible; his suffering for us was outlined for humanity. In our case, following Jesus Christ implies a cross associated with the purpose for which he calls us, he chooses us. Each one according to his call, big or small cross depends on the call, but, following Jesus always implies sacrifice, above all, we need to crucify our will to fulfill God's plans.

After giving my whole life to Jesus Christ, I began to serve him, advancing, fulfilling his task, my purpose, I feel totally protected. With the experiences, I learned not to cling to my life. Every day I give my life to God to save it, even, to save it, literally, He saved me twice.

One night, in a dream, I saw a man place his gun on my head, but, just before shooting, God didn't allow it, he saved me. When I woke up, I heard:

That will happen —said God in my heart.

After crying, when I calmed down, He asked:

—Why are you crying? You saw it, they won't kill you.

Several days passed without suspecting who, how, when, where, why, would happen. I had no idea.

Suddenly, one night, while driving, two armed men crossed and they pointed to my son and me. I thought about overwhelming them (thought of the devil), but, immediately I remembered the dream, I stopped, lower the windows, two pointed to us, three climbed into the car, and I saw two more. They hit me over the head, and when the guy was going to shoot me, I screamed:

—God.

Immediately, that guy and his henchmen (seven in total), ran away, running, nor the police or anyone come. It happened as in the Bible, Moses said:

"The Lord will overcome your enemies when they attack you. They will come out to attack you from one direction, but they will scatter by seven! "

When advancing in the car, my seven—year—old son said:

—Papa, let's go back to kill them all.

Without caring about the loneliness and darkness of the place, I remembered the biblical importance of forgiveness, without hesitation, I felt the need to stop and pray for them.

Let's pray, forgive them — I said to my son.

The boy and I pray in the same place where it happened, we forgive them. That night, we sleep in peace, from that experience my son only remembers:

—Don't cry little boy, don't cry.

The next night, in the church, I understood why God allowed that situation. Until that moment, I was trying to get directly to God the Father, bypassing Jesus Christ. I knew the gospels, but I was deceived. I didn't seek God the Father through God the Son. That's why, that night in the church, Jesus placed his hand on my shoulder and whispered in my ear:

—Not even a single day of your life, never forget, you only reach God the Father through me.

Some might think that Jesus threatened me; I didn't feel it that way. He loves us, he always warns us.

In his grace and mercy, Jesus didn't allow that man to shoot me. Here only happens what God allows to happen. The devil cannot defeat us; we ourselves lose when we disobey the will of God. God had shown me how I would be saved; trying to overwhelm the subjects would have been a mistake of irrevocable consequence. Trust him.

With that gun in my head, although I was distressed and holding my son's hand I felt peace in my heart. My spirit knew my eternal destiny, I believe it so. If the guy fired, I would go to heaven.

Otherwise, the day of the accident, this time I went to hell.

It wasn't in God's purpose to let me die that day, but, the devil knows my purpose. Always try to kill me. I am protected as long as I obey Jesus, I love him with all my heart, I love my neighbor, I forgive everyone and I repent if I sin.

In the Bible, we can read in proverbs "above all things take care of your heart, because it determines the direction of your life". Solomon wrote it.

Christians recognize the obvious sins, the sins of the flesh, but, we ignore invisible sins, that is, some sins of the heart.

For example, getting drunk is an easy sin to identify, Christians know, that doesn't please God. It's easier to deal with alcohol addiction than with lack of forgiveness, pride, arrogance, haughtiness, self—centeredness, vainglory, rebelliousness; those "invisible" sins are rooted in the heart.

These sins of the heart may predominate in the church over those visible or easy to identify. When Satan recognizes that he has no valid arguments to kill us, then he tries to attack, dirty, hurt people's hearts because those sins are harder to recognize.

We are at war — I heard in my heart say the Spirit of the Lord, good versus evil.

In general, without details, in the spiritual world they have information. As Satan knows part of our purpose for God, then:

First, try to prevent you from fulfilling your call. Satan took advantage of my mistakes when I committed adultery, that sin left me temporarily disabled (lame), four herniated discs in my spine. Then, in the traffic accident he tried to kill me, or at least leave me prostrate in a bed for life, or in a wheelchair, sought to prevent a purpose that even I didn't know. What purpose? To run for Jesus. He knew that years later God would send me to run for Jesus Christ. Until that moment, I wasn't saved; I had not received Jesus in my heart. To have died after that, without a doubt, I would have gone to hell.

Second, being saved, and fulfilling my purpose for Jesus, Satan tried to kill me through the armed man. Since I couldn't get to hell, because I was saved, then, he sought to get me out of the war; he didn't care if I went to heaven with such and stop doing my work of salvation on earth.

Third, recognizing my salvation now attempts to harm my heart through situations, including with my family. In a dream, I understood how my descendants and wife can die if I don't fulfill my call. God warned me: "never escape your purpose" —said Jesus in my heart, upon awakening.

In short, Satan tries to kill you to receive you in hell, if you are not saved, but have a purpose for

God. If you are saved, tries to limit yourself to impede your purpose, the call of Jesus Christ; If he doesn't succeed then he seeks to kill you so that you don't influence spiritual warfare. Finally, since Satan doesn't have valid arguments to limit yourself or kill yourself, then seeks to sow sin in your heart. There it's more difficult to identify sin, and if we let it grow, a sin of the heart has a hard root to tear.

Although the blood of Jesus Christ cleanses us, the roots of sins can continue in our spirit, tempting us to sin. From experience I know. Adultery I inherited from my ancestors, grandparents. My father repeated that disobedience to God, now he must repent, for his eternal welfare, he needs to ask for forgiveness; I, without knowing the spiritual world, also committed adultery. I repented and I pardoned, I managed to free myself, but, I cannot trust myself. Jesus Christ warns me, women can be my weak point. In my family, we must defeat the spirit of adultery; we can prevent our children from repeating that mistake.

The consequences on my son could be worse. Whoever is given more, more will be required, we can read it in the Bible. The little one knows my testimony, knows that God abhors divorce. He knows the word of God; he cannot claim ignorance, so now he is more responsible for his mistakes. In my case, I only knew, from the Catholic Church, a commandment that says: You shall not covet your neighbor's wife.

Satan thinks he will beat God and the attack on the army of Jesus Christ is imminent. Men can be attacked with beautiful women, and women with attractive men. As there are spiritual gifts that Jesus gives us, there are also evil gifts of Satan for their own. We are in the middle of a spiritual war, and Christians are more warned than others.

We can read it in the Gospel of Luke: "someone who does not know and does something wrong, will be punished slightly. Someone who has been given much, much will be asked in return; and someone who has been entrusted a lot, even more will be required. "

Every Christian is required more; we know the truth of the word of God. In no other is there salvation, only in Jesus, there is no other name under heaven, given to men, in which we can be saved, we know it. We know of Adam's sin, but, God reconciled us to Him through Jesus.

We are required more to those who have received the unmerited mercy of God, in difficult circumstances of our lives, who receive miracles.

When Jesus Christ began to open my spiritual eyes and ears I understood some details of my past, above all, I verified that God was always by my side, loving me, protecting me. For example, in the traffic accident I had multiple fractures of the right humerus, that is, in my arm.

I learned several lessons from that experience. Before entering the operating room, hours after the impact, the doctor in charge told me:

—Luis, surgery is risky, you must authorize me.

On his face I read "you can lose your arm."

God bless you, proceed —I answered crying.

I had never said "God bless you" to anyone besides my son and nephews. That night I received another miracle, the doctors managed to rebuild my arm and I completely recovered the mobility and sensitivity, I only lost strength, then I recovered it with therapies.

However, I have a scar all along the humerus. Although I used healing creams, the brand never diminished, not even a little. Then, I appreciated that memory on my arm as a reminder of the mercy of God with me and of Jesus' love.

But, that revelation went further. Since I was a child, on my face, on my lip, I have a scar that was impossible to eliminate. One day, I asked Jesus for that memory, and about it He answered me:

—When you look in the mirror you can remember that I was with you as a child, protecting you, loving you, you and I know what happened that afternoon, it wasn't worse, I saved you. Before you were born, I set you apart for me.

Jesus Christ loved us first, He always loves us.

Even in hell, Jesus felt sorry for the souls who suffer eternally; He loves them. God the Father also loves you. Therefore, they warn us so much, let's take care of salvation, and let's avoid hell.

Among so many cases, the servant of God saw in hell a woman to whom Jesus healed of cancer. On earth, when He healed her, he told her not to sin anymore because something worse could happen to her. She tried to follow him, but, seeing that those who preach the word of God are not popular, she preferred the approval of the people over the approval of Jesus. She forgot her miracle, she left Christian friends and although she never had the intention of losing herself, Satan possessed her, she suffered on earth more than before. In her heart she heard, God called her. She planned to return to Jesus, He waited for her but, she died before.

That is one of the great deceptions in churches, Christians who being aware of sin, plan to repent later, and that day never comes.

Another case caused special attention in me. The servant of God saw a woman suffering in hell because she worshiped Hindu gods and idols, she didn't believe in the gospel. When she died, she cried out to those gods asking for salvation, but nobody could help her.

That case is obvious, people like that end up in hell, we Christians know it. The reflection in my heart was this: the adoration of virgins and saints is also idolatry, even if they were remarkable people, we, only, must worship God.

Thousands of people worship alleged apparitions of virgins when the Bible clearly mentions that Satan disguises himself as an angel of light. These apparitions don't mention Jesus Christ, they cannot, in fact, many of them have not even been mentioned anywhere. Human beings are easily deceived by the supernatural, I know from experience. In my adolescence I saw diabolical manifestations, reading letters, regressions, Santeria, spiritual things; and I don't deny it, they exist, but, all of them come from evil, they are tricks of Satan to deceive us.

As you can appreciate, dear readers, I am not a Christian raised within the true gospel, but a sinner rescued from hell. Therefore, every night I try to remember the teaching of Jesus, who spoke of trust in our own righteousness and stressed contempt for others. I summarize the story:

Two men went to the temple to pray. One was a Pharisee, and the other was a despised tax collector. The Pharisee, standing apart from the others, made the following prayer: "I thank you, God, that I am not a sinner like everyone else. Well, I don't cheat, I don't sin and I don't commit adultery. I'm not like that tax collector at all! I fast twice a week and I give you the tithe of my income. "Instead, the tax collector stood at a distance and didn't even dare to look up at the sky while praying, but instead hit his chest in pain as he said: "God, have mercy on me, because I am a sinner"

I tell you that it was this sinner — and not the Pharisee — who returned home justified before God, Jesus explained with forcefulness, before telling them:

—For those who exalt themselves will be humbled, and those who humble themselves will be exalted.

Likewise, the Apostle Paul wrote in Galatians: "Well, if you pretend to be righteous before God by fulfilling the law, you have been separated from Christ! They have fallen from the grace of God. "

The preaching of grace without repentance, has deceived men and women, Satan hides how we can fall from the grace of God.

If God is a Spirit, he must be worshiped in Spirit and in truth. We must aim to be saints because He is holy. The Bible is clear, the writer to the Hebrews said: "Strive to live in peace with all and strive to lead a holy life, because those who are not saints will not see the Lord."

That is, without holiness no one will see the Lord.

The struggle for the soul of Christians is constant but at our disposal we have the weapons to overcome spiritually. In hell, the servant of God heard that many demons said:

—We have to watch carefully those who believe in Jesus, because they can throw us out. When we hear the name of Jesus, we have to flee.

In this regard, in hell Jesus told the servant:

— My angels protect my people from these evil spirits and their work does not prosper against them. I also protect many who are not saved, although they do not know it. I have many angels employed to prevent the evil plans of Satan. I have all power in heaven and on earth. Do not fear Satan; fear God.

Inside and outside the churches, the spiritual battle is a reality. This book was written as a warning to sons and daughters of God, not to unbelievers. Only our Lord Jesus Christ knows those who will give them wisdom to understand that we can lose salvation. To millions because a revival is coming; Spiritual warfare depends on congregations. The church, Christians, depends on caring for salvation. Let's get out of the deception, we stop thinking that "once saved, always saved", because it's not true, that lie comes from Satan. We can lose our salvation by not repenting or forgiving. Believers who lead a double life must repent and follow the right path, while they are still on time.

Remember the letter to Hebrews where it says: "The Lord will judge his own people."

If the unbelievers need to repent, much more we believers to whom the blood of Jesus Christ redeemed us — which made us saints — we cannot despise the Holy Spirit that convicts us for the grace and mercy of God.

God gives me what I DON'T deserve

None of us deserve salvation. By his grace, God gives us the opportunity to be saved.

In the churches belonging to the body of Christ, the Spirit notices that the end is near and Jesus Christ is calling sinners to repent and be saved. Therefore, a global revival is planned, growth in the preaching of the gospel. Millions of new disciples, of all nations, will be baptized in the name of the Father and the Son and the Holy Spirit. God always wins, is prophesied.

If for God salvation depended on deserving then we would all be destined to hell. If God gave us what we deserve, then, we would receive punishment that is what we deserve, without exception, all of us, sin, in one way or another.

Therefore, while the human being was still weak, in his time, Jesus Christ died for all sinners.

God showed us his love that in being sinners, disobedient to his will, Jesus Christ died for us. That we must always remember so as not to believe ourselves just and saved by our own opinion.

As we mentioned, hell was created for Satan and his henchmen. What shall we say then? That there's injustice in God? No way!

God has mercy on which He decides to have mercy and God has compassion on which He decides to have compassion. It doesn't depend on us but on God, who, out of love, has mercy.

In Jesus Christ we have redemption through his blood; and forgiveness of our sins according to the riches of his grace. That is a reality, but that doesn't disregard the need for repentance.

The apostle Paul, an example of repentance, confessed in his first letter to Timothy:

—Jesus Christ came into the world to save sinners, of which I am the worst of all. But God had mercy on me, so that Jesus would use me as the prime example of his great patience even with the worst sinners. In that way, others will realize that they can also believe in Him and receive eternal life.

The apostle understood our Lord Jesus Christ loves us. God, our Father, loves us. That is why he gave us eternal consolation and good hope, by grace. This grace of God has been manifested, bringing salvation to all men through Jesus.

As Christians, we know it. By grace, God saved us, never by our righteous actions, by his mercy. We know, Jesus Christ washed us, taking away our sins, gave us a new birth and new life through the Holy Spirit. Every Christian who knows the word of God knows it.

If God gives me what I don't deserve (salvation), then should every Christian take care of his salvation? Of course, until the last breath, let's read why.

Remember "Christian" is a person who by faith received Christ in his heart, trusts him as the only, sufficient savior, and follows him. Attending a Christian church doesn't make me a Christian. Being born and growing up in a Christian family doesn't make me a Christian either. In the bible, we can read how, in Antioch, for the first time, believers were called "Christians". That's where "Christians" come from, it's by following Christ.

Is the preaching of grace necessary in the churches? Of course! When we believe, God saves us by his grace. But, we have no merit in that, we must admit it. Salvation is God's gift, as a gift, we must appreciate it and take care of it.

Salvation is not a reward for good things we have done. None of us can boast of being saved by merit. Therefore, I insist, we must appreciate the salvation and, above all, take care of it.

When we receive Jesus Christ we are new creatures, old things have passed, all are made new. By faith we believe it and the bible supports it in the second letter to the Corinthians. From my own experience, I recognize the changes in me, after receiving Jesus Christ.

Myself, I am the first surprised of the new me. Without God I am nothing, I admit it. If all those changes in me happened, and still happen, through salvation, it's obvious, I need to take care of it.

The apostle Peter, in his first letter, taught us how "we were rescued from our vain way of life, which we received from our parents; not with corruptible things, like gold or silver, but with the precious blood of Christ, as of a lamb without blemish and without contamination." Therefore, if the price for my salvation was the blood of Jesus Christ, it's a gift of incalculable value; the most valuable gift I can receive. We must appreciate salvation.

From the Apostle Paul, from his letter to the Romans we can learn: we are justified, then, by faith, we have peace with God through our Lord Jesus Christ. Every true Christian recognizes the peace that is felt in being reconciled with God. That is something inexplicable, it's a peace that surpasses all understanding, worth appreciating and caring.

In addition to all those enjoyable arguments on earth, through our salvation, we also need to take care of it to receive the glorification, and the complete reward, in eternal life.

The earthly struggle for souls is real. Until the end, Satan will try to lose our salvation. It's preferable and wiser to take care of it, than to trust us.

Certainly, sin is no longer our master, because we no longer live under the demands of the law of Moses, we live in the freedom of God's grace. That is true, that freedom allows you to avoid sin. On the other hand, when sin was our master, for us it was more difficult, or impossible, to avoid sinning.

For example, a Christian who suffered from an addiction can recognize how this addiction was his master over his will. By being free, by the grace of God, we manage to overcome all those spiritual bonds and avoid those sins. Without breaking such ties, it's impossible to overcome addiction.

From experience, I know. As a result of the separation of my son, as a result of the divorce, I fell into alcoholism. The only way to sleep, and have some peace, was intoxicating me. One Sunday, I felt the desire to cross the street and go to the Christian church in front of my house. That morning, I received Jesus Christ as my Lord and Savior. Upon leaving the temple, someone gave me a small book with the Gospel of John. When I arrived at my house, I placed that book on the table, next to the liquor bottles.

When night came, when I went to get drunk to sleep, I saw the little book and for a moment, I hesitate between pouring me a drink of whiskey or reading the book. At the time, without understanding anything, simply, I felt more desire to read, than to drink.

Suddenly, reading it I fell asleep, since that day I managed to avoid alcohol. Receive peace by reading the word of God, the Bible.

Among the arguments, of those who affirm that salvation cannot be lost, is the verse "there is no condemnation for those who belong to Christ Jesus; and because you belong to Him, the power of the Spirit who gives life has set you free from the power of sin, which leads to death."

The power of the Holy Spirit frees us from the power of sin, only then, we are strong to overcome it. That doesn't indicate that God likes us to sin; God doesn't like to see us outside of His will. Jesus doesn't condemn us, he loves us, but we condemn ourselves by practicing sin. Because we are Christians, saved, we believe that we can lead a double life before God and that is a deception of Satan.

As I advanced in the service to Jesus Christ, I began to have visions, that is, awake; Something different from dreams while I sleep. One day, I had a simple vision, I began to see myself as a child of about three years old, sitting on Jesus' legs. At the time, God the Father and the Holy Spirit appeared in the vision. To this day, depending on the circumstances, I see myself closer to some of them, something simple, with Jesus at the right hand of the Father and Holy Spirit in front of them.

I have never seen the throne of God, in that vision, simply, I see those three people, of whom, Jesus and God the Father are sitting, I see the Holy Spirit standing. I see the face of God the Father as light, and I don't detail Jesus' face, but I feel its presence.

If I believed that salvation isn't lost, perhaps that revelation could guide me to abuse grace, to do with my life what I wanted, but no. From that vision, I feel more responsibility and tried not to sadden God, Jesus or the Holy Spirit. In that vision I approached them, I enjoy their love, I talk to them, I repent, I embrace them, I enjoy their love.

At first I thought it was my imagination. Then I read, in the Bible, how the Apostle Paul explained: "He raised us from the dead (referring to God) together with Christ and we sat with Him in the heavenly places, because we are united to Christ Jesus."

The greater intimacy with God the Father, Jesus Christ and the greater Holy Spirit is our commitment to them. He tried to obey them in everything; his will is the best for me, my family, and for all of us.

Christians can approach the throne of grace with confidence to receive mercy, and find grace for timely help. We must remember it.

We can never take advantage of the grace to sin premeditatedly or to justify our sins already committed. The children of God know his word, the

Bible, we know that he likes God, and that he dislikes him. We need to take advantage of grace, but, to repent and receive timely forgiveness.

If we are wrong, and we sin, and then we can take advantage of the grace of God, I insist, always to repent, ask for forgiveness and be forgiven.

Before sleeping, I apologize to God and repent for the sins committed. That helps me keep my heart cleaner. The Holy Spirit helps, He reminds me if, consciously or unconsciously, I spoke, I thought, or I did something unpleasant before God, or if I failed to do His will. Knowing God's will in something, and not doing it, is sin by omission.

God DOESN'T give me what I deserve

Our sins can be in thoughts, words, deeds or omission. Not to heed Jesus' call, not to fulfill his purpose, is to omit his will.

God doesn't give me what I deserve, that is, punishment. Through Jesus, God allows us to repent. Although we deserve punishment, all genuine repentance leads to forgiveness. Here, you may wonder why you insist so much on repentance? Because in all the cases mentioned, of Christians in hell, none of them repented in time, a grave error.

In my personal opinion, I believe that, had they sincerely repented, even before their last breath on earth, God would have forgiven them all. God is merciful. Let us remember some verses from the letter of the Apostle Paul to the Romans:

"But because you are stubborn and refuse to turn from your sin, you are storing up terrible punishment for yourself; for a day of anger is coming, when God's righteous judgment will be revealed. He will judge everyone according to what they have done. He will give eternal life to those who keep on doing good, seeking after the glory and honor and immortality that God offers. But he will pour out his anger and wrath on those who live for themselves, who refuse to obey the truth and instead live lives of wickedness.

There will be trouble and calamity for everyone who keeps on doing what is evil. "

From these verses we can emphasize two important aspects. The first, "eternal life to those who continue doing well", to follow implies continuity in doing well until the last day of our life; who defines good? Only God, never ourselves. The second aspect is "anger over those who live for themselves". When a Christian prefers to make his wishes, above the wishes of Jesus, gives Satan opportunity to sow a root of rebellion in his heart, which, if not identified in time, can lead to spiritual death, and then to the earthly. We need to seek the will of God in absolutely everything.

In my case, even to eat a chewing gum I look for the direction of God, why? out of his will that gum can cause a caries, and if I don't detect it in time, for that caries I can lose my teeth. The same happens with rebellion, it begins as something minimal, without realizing we leave the will of God, we think that we are well when in reality we are being deceived by Satan. We need absolute obedience to God.

Recently, there were fuel problems in the city where I live. Faced with that situation, I asked God where to go, because, my tank was almost empty.

Go across! Leave your friend at home, put gasoline near your home —I heard in my heart.

However, my friend reminded me that if I continued straight there was a fuel station nearby.

Although I recognize the need to seek the will of God in everything, I thought "God told me to go across but there is nothing wrong to go straight; anyway, I don't believe it's a sin, if God sent me to cross it is because that station is closed"

I keep straight. As expected, the station was closed. However, arriving at my friend's house, I checked again because I must seek the will of God in everything. At an intersection, a man with a gun in his hand is in front of me. Because of the mercy of Jesus, nothing happened, just the scare.

On the way to my house I asked God why did you allow that scare? — And I heard in my heart:

—You should have obeyed me, if you went across, you would have avoided it.

The will of Jesus is the best for us. God suffers because of the consequences of disobeying Him. If God suffers with our suffering on earth, he suffers the most when he sees his sons or daughters in hell. He always warns us, and here he is warning us. We must take care of salvation, we can lose it. Don't abuse grace, if we sin, let's repent.

Sin means disobedience to the will of God. If at that time God sent me to go across and I went straight, so what did I do? Well, sin. For my sake, I felt the need to ask God for forgiveness for that. Many will see it as insignificant and exaggerated. Since I want Jesus to take care of me in everything, I need to repent and obey Him in everything.

Jesus Christ is not a dictator, he is our Lord.

One weekend day, when I woke up, I asked him, "Sir, should I train? To the heart, He answered me:

—I'm not a dictator. What do you want to do today?

I don't know; what should I do? — I replied.

Today you don't want to train — added Jesus.

Little by little, I evolved spiritually to only obey God out of fear, to obey God out of fear and convenience, that morning I discovered him. It's different for God to give us the option to choose him to command us to do something and disobey.

A true Christian needs to be obedient and not continue living an immoral life. In his first letter the apostle John wrote: "Anyone who continues to live in him will not sin. But anyone who keeps on sinning does not know him or understand who he is." Immorality is defined by God, never by us. We must know his word, be intimate with him.

Likewise, a true Christian never fails to congregate. "These people left our churches, but they never really belonged with us; otherwise they would have stayed with us. When they left, it proved that they did not belong with us." we can read that too, in the first letter of John. Jesus Christ can move us as a congregation but he always wants to gather us.

Without the necessary revelation, the Bible can be used by Satan to deceive us. Remember, when Satan tempted Jesus, he used the scriptures. Another of the biblical passages used by those who say that once saved we are always saved, is in the letter of the Apostle Paul to the Romans:

"And I am convinced that nothing can ever separate us from God's love. Neither death nor life, neither angels nor demons, neither our fears for today nor our worries about tomorrow—not even the powers of hell can separate us from God's love. No power in the sky above or in the earth below— indeed, nothing in all creation will ever be able to separate us from the love of God that is revealed in Christ Jesus our Lord." Certainly nothing can separate us from the love of God. Therefore, God warns us about hell. God is a loving Father but he is also a Just Judge. From the letter of Judas, too, we can read:

"Now to Him who is able to keep you from stumbling and to present you unblemished in His glorious presence, with great joy— to the only God our Savior be glory, majesty, dominion, and authority, through Jesus Christ our Lord, before all time, and now, and for all eternity. Amen."

God is powerful to keep us from falling and to present ourselves without blemish before his glory, but it's we ourselves who can turn away from Jesus and live outside the will of God. He doesn't force us; we must remain by his side.

From the letter to the Romans we know that just as sin reined over all and led to death, now the wonderful grace of God reigns, which puts us in the right relationship with Him and results in eternal life; through Jesus Christ our Lord.

In the book of events, we are taught how we need to repent and become Jesus so that our sins may be erased, so that times of refreshment may come from the presence of the Lord. Repentance appears throughout the Bible.

When we receive Jesus Christ our sins are forgiven, but, as we continue our life, we continue to sin consciously or unconsciously. The servant of God also traveled to heaven. There she saw that each of us had his own record book where what we do was written but also saw how the blood of Jesus Christ cleansed our sins written in those books.

Therefore, we must repent in a timely manner; let us take advantage of the blood of Jesus Christ for the forgiveness of our sins. When we receive Jesus Christ all our sins are erased from those record books in heaven. That doesn't mean that our future sins will be automatically erased, if we sin, we need to repent in a timely manner. Whoever thinks that because he received Jesus Christ can lead a life away from God and sin, without suffering consequences, is being deceived by Satan.

From the time of Jesus on earth, He preached the good news of God without neglecting the need for repentance. The time promised by God has finally arrived! —Jesus announced— The kingdom of God is near! Repent of your sins and create the Good News!

Some churches replaced repentance with an unbalanced preaching of grace. Weak Christians fall into those deceptions of Satan. They think that to say Jesus to Jesus is enough. They believe that they can lead an unpleasant life before God, without suffering eternal consequences.

When the apostle Peter preached the gospel, many asked him and the other apostles:

—Brothers, what should we do?

Pedro replied:

—Each one of you must repent of your sins and return to God, be baptized in the name of Jesus Christ for the forgiveness of your sins. Then, you will receive the gift of the Holy Spirit.

From the first church, to the present one, Christianity became a religion when it stopped believing in the Holy Spirit. If Jesus needed the Holy Spirit to operate on Earth, why would we, being sinners, not need Him even more? Without the Holy Spirit we can be deceived by Satan. All Christians depend on the Holy Spirit.

The Holy Spirit guides us, is our inseparable friend, but also reproves us when necessary. The sadness that is according to the will of God produces repentance that leads to salvation; but, the sadness of the world produces death. We can read it in the letter to the Corinthians.

Repentance can lead us to humiliation; remember the following promise written in the Bible:

"If my people, who bear my name, humble themselves and pray, seek my face and turn away from their perverse conduct, I will hear from heaven, forgive their sins and restore their land."

How we see that promise is for the people of God, not for the unbelievers. Those who conceal their sins will not prosper, but those who confess them, abandon them, find mercy. That statement is also biblical. We must always repent.

If we confess our sins, God is faithful and just to forgive us and to cleanse us from all unrighteousness. Confessing disobedience, in addition to forgiveness, can bring liberation so as not to repeat them. Having ignored the times of ignorance, God now declares all men, everywhere, to repent, and as Christians that includes us even more. We must clean the heart.

The wages of sin is death, but the gift of God is eternal life; Jesus Christ our Lord.

The second letter of Peter we can read: "The Lord is not slow concerning His promise, as some count slowness. But He is patient with us, because He does not want any to perish, but all to come to repentance. "

I know God's patience with us. As I remember my past, and move forward every day, I admit it. The warnings can be to complete churches. For example, in apocalypse, he took these three cases:

First, in the message to the church in Ephesus, you are warned that God knows everything you do, among the good things is your hard work and patience with perseverance, suffering for the name of Jesus and patience without giving up. But, God had a complaint against them, they didn't love God or love each other like they did at the beginning. For that reason, he ordered them "Go back to me and do the works that you did at the beginning. If you do not repent, I will come and remove your candelabrum from your place among the churches." Repentance was indispensable for that church.

Second, in the message to the church of Sardis, the Lord made them know "I know everything you do and that you have the reputation of being alive, but you are dead. Wake up! Strengthen what little you have left, because even what is left is about to die. I see that your actions do not meet the requirements of my God. Go back to everything you heard and believed at the beginning, and hold it firmly. "

Likewise, the warning came over that church: "Repent and return to me. If you do not wake up, I will come to you suddenly, when you least expect it, as a thief does. "However, God recognized that some in the church of Sardis had not stained their clothes with evil and he promised them that they would walk with Him with me dressed in white, because they are worthy. Finally, he announced to them that all those who come out victors will be dressed in white and He would never erase their names from the book of life, but announce before the Father and his angels that they belong to him. As we read, our names can be erased from the book of life, we can lose salvation.

Third, in the message to the church in Laodicea, the Lord informed them: "I know everything you do, that you are neither cold nor hot. How I wish you were the one or the other! but since you are warm, neither cold nor hot, I will spit you out of my mouth! You say: I'm rich, I have everything I want, I do not need anything! "And you do not realize that you are an unhappy and a miser; you are poor, blind and you are naked. I correct and discipline all those I love.

Therefore, be diligent and repent of your indifference. Look! I am at the door and I call. If you hear my voice and open the door, I will go in and have dinner together as friends. All those who come out victors will sit with me on my throne, just as I came out victorious and sat down with my Father on his throne. "We see again the need for repentance as a way to access salvation and intimacy with Jesus Christ.

Finally, those messages ended with the phrase "Everyone who has ears to hear must listen to the Spirit and understand what He says to the churches." Just like them, we need to listen to the Holy Spirit with our spiritual ears because only through Him; we recognize the truth.

Likewise, as God forgives us, we need and we must forgive others. From the Bible we know that if our brother in Christ sins, we can rebuke him with love, and if he repents we should forgive him; as many times as he repents we must forgive him. As we have seen before, any lack of forgiveness can damage our hearts. Forgiving is an indispensable matter.

Christians sometimes forget that Jesus said:

—The healthy have no need of a doctor, but those who are sick do. I have not come to call the righteous, but sinners to repentance.

To be fair is to be fair in God's opinion, never from my own criteria. If Jesus calls us daily, it's because something of sinners still finds us, but He, who began the good work in us, will continue it until it is completely finished. Let's not allow the entrance of Satan's deceptions; we are all still sinners in some area of our life. We have not yet been perfected, we need to repent, we can sin daily without knowing it. Let's take care of salvation because we can lose it.

My intention is not to make a judgment against anyone; on the contrary, the desire of my heart is to highlight the goodness of God, who leads us to repentance.

Don't you realize how kind, tolerant and patient God is with us? It doesn't that matter in our hearts? Don't we see how the goodness of God is to guide us to repent and abandon all sin? In one of his letters, the apostle Paul explained it to the Romans, it's biblical.

Some people claim to be fair and not be lost, it's possible, I do not deny it; but, most of us are sheep of the best Shepherd, Jesus Christ, who in the parable of the lost sheep, taught us: "If a man has a hundred sheep and one of them is lost, what will he do? Will not he leave the other ninety-nine in the desert and go out and find the lost until he finds it? And, when he finds it, he will carry it with joy on his shoulders and take it home. When he arrives, he will call his friends and neighbors and tell them: "Rejoice with me because I found my lost sheep."

There is more joy in heaven for a lost sinner who repents and returns to God than for ninety-nine righteous people who didn't go astray! "

Dear reader, that lost sheep, that sinner, without suspecting it, can be a Christian. We need intimacy with God to be totally sure that we are righteous before Him and have no sins. For my part, I prefer not to trust myself and receive their forgiveness, to repent, when I sin, in anything.

This book was written for Christians, believers, followers of Jesus Christ, not for unbelievers. The warnings here are for the people of God; men, women, imperfect families used by the perfect God. Who thought himself perfect; Lucifer was expelled from heaven and, now, is in hell.

Any of us can lose their salvation by trusting, Satan, who believes himself to be perfect, can deceive us to ignore our mistakes. We all sin in something, major or minor sins, consciously or unconsciously, we disobey the will of God, even in detail. We depend on the spirit of humility to recognize our sins, ask for forgiveness, and repent in a timely manner.

God said that David had a heart according to his. If that king sinned several times, he killed, he committed adultery. We have asked ourselves: What was special about him?

The secret of King David's heart was: when he sinned, he repented. Otherwise, King Saul sinned, less than David, but he didn't repent in time.

Saul died in suicide, David died in healthy old age.

Christian, brother or sister, as you read these lines, imagine that I speak to you in person. I love you with all my heart, whether I know you or not; if Jesus Christ is your only Lord and Savior, then you are my brother. God has warned me several times, every Christian can lose his salvation; we must take care of it. We need to repent, for grace, and, forgive, for grace.

That warning is light in the dark. Jesus Christ is lighting his light of understanding among the deceptions of Satan within the Christian churches. He lights his light to seek us, as he explained in the parable of the lost coin, He said:

—Suppose a woman has ten silver coins and loses one. Will not she light a lamp and sweep the entire house and search carefully until she finds it? And, when she finds it, she will call her friends and neighbors and she will say: "Rejoice with me because I found my lost coin!" In the same way, there is joy in the presence of the angels of God when a single sinner repents.

In Christians, the lost sheep represents someone who moved away from Jesus; currency loss, is who is lost, even, within the congregation.

The deception of Satan, with the preaching of grace without repentance, is darkness within the church.

The grace of God is not a permission to lead an unpleasant lifestyle before Him, far from Jesus.

The blood of Jesus Christ is sacred, it cost him his life, he redeemed us and erased our sins, but, that doesn't indicate that it erases our disobedience to God, current or future, we need to repent.

Grace never allows you to lead a double life. That is, being a Christian in the temple, obeying God in the church, and then, outside the church, leading a life far from Jesus. That is serious, God knows everything.

I don't want you to die, says the Sovereign Lord. Change course and live! That warning is biblical; we can read it in the book of Ezekiel.

In the Bible, in the book of Joel, we can read one of the most powerful calls to repentance:

Therefore, the Lord says: "Return to me now, while there is time; give me your heart."

The need for repentance, daily, within the churches is mainly due to sins of the heart. The sins of the flesh are evident in Christians, but the sinful stains in the heart are the hardest and most difficult to identify.

As I wrote this book, each night, before going to sleep, I felt the need to ask God for a deep cleansing of my heart, to eliminate any generational or acquired dirt in my sins.

In dreams, God showed me areas of my heart where there is still concupiscence, the roots of sins that have not been completely uprooted.

For example, years ago Jesus Christ showed me his willingness to reconcile with my wife. I conquered fornication and decided to remain alone because He would bring her back. However, in one of those dreams when I was accompanied by a beautiful woman, I thought: I am going to sleep with her, but since I must not to fool her, because she is a Christian, then I tell her that Jesus wants me to get back together with my wife.

Being asleep I knew, I felt, that was wrong. With that dream I understood, there is a sinful root of fornication, which I must tear out of my heart. I see the beautiful woman in the church and I have never said anything insinuating to her. The dream served as a warning and, perhaps, liberation, I must not trust myself, I can fall.

All those nights, before sleeping, pray, and, in spiritual vision I saw myself as the little boy of three years, but, sleeping in the chest of God the Father. Every night I had different dreams where I saw the reality of my spirit, current sinful roots, and temptations contrary to the will of God. In some cases, I received liberation and overcame the temptation. In others, I almost fell into temptation. In a few, I failed the exam, there is still much cleaning in my heart.

After the dream with the beautiful lady of the church, I continued asking God to cleanse my heart. The next night, I had the following dream: In one room we were a friend athlete and I totally alone. While I was lying down she walked in front of me, contouring her buttocks, wearing a small bikini. When I saw her (still asleep), I thought "I'm going to look for her husband". She came back and stood in front of me, totally naked, as an athlete her body was spectacular. However, I saw her without lust or sexual desires. I just said, "Go find your husband."

Before, such an erotic dream would have ended up in a pornographic film, asleep. We need to be purified by God, we will always be tempted.

These two dreams are examples. Before receiving Jesus Christ, and even months after advancing in the gospel, asleep, I discovered sinful roots that I didn't even suspect. Cases mentioned, in previous books. Jesus wants to free us, He wants to perfect us, but we must give him the heart so that God can purify him with his fire.

Trust us; it's a serious mistake as Christians. Satan is on the lookout. Any sinful root can grow into a serious sin. We need to clean it in time. Christians never disobey God premeditatedly, we know the consequences. Who sins, he does it trusting in valid arguments according to his own opinion. Now, grace is being used as an argument for not repenting when sinning; that is a deception of Satan.

From the Bible: "God is not a man, he does not lie. He is not human; he does not change his mind. Did he ever speak without acting? Did he ever promise something without fulfilling?"

God promises salvation, but we must take care of it. Every day, we need intimacy with Jesus to enjoy the promises of God; He is merciful and compassionate, slow to get angry and full of love. Before punishing, God sent Jonah to warn them: "And God saw what they did, that they turned from their evil way; and he repented of the evil he had said he would do to them, and he did not do it." God is willing to desist, not to punish. When we turn from the wrong way, God can repent of the punishment.

Is knowing Jesus Christ enough?

There is a God and a Mediator who can reconcile humanity with God, and it's Jesus Christ.

Reaching God the Father is impossible without knowing Jesus, we know it. But to know him is enough?

Remember, from the Gospel of John, how, Jesus, while looking at the sky, said:

—And the way to have eternal life is to know you, the only true God, and Jesus Christ, whom you sent to earth.

Knowing Jesus is essential, Christians long for a relationship with him. But is it enough?

I will try to explain it in the following way:

If by faith, we receive Jesus in our hearts, and by faith we are made children of God, then, by faith, we begin to belong to the family of God. So far, I think, no Christian has doubts. God is our Father and Jesus Christ our brother.

However, in every family its members have responsibilities according to their age and maturity. Thus, as in earthly life we begin as children, spiritually as well. By receiving Jesus, we are adopted children of God, spiritual babies.

In the earthly, after being babies we move on to children, adolescents, adults, and elderly. In the spiritual is the same, we start immature and get mature according to the role model in Christian formation. In the congregation through pastors, leaders, brothers, always remembering, the main role model is Jesus. He showed us the nice lifestyle before God.

In my case, I met my brother when he was seventeen years old, I never suspected his existence. The next day, from my dad to introduce me, I think, if someone had asked me, do you know your brother? Maybe I would have answered, yes, although it could be false. Knowing someone implies something beyond seeing, hearing or speaking to him, once or several times.

In a similar way it happens with Jesus Christ.

We hear of Jesus Christ, by images, perhaps, we have an idea of his appearance. Now, if someone asks us, do you know Jesus? We are we really prepared to respond?

With lightness and in Latin American countries much more, we believe we know someone because we saw him once or we shared a day with that person.

In my personal opinion, we really get to know someone when we live with him or her for a while. It happens the same way with Jesus Christ. Only live with Him, have intimacy with Him, the Holy Spirit helps us to know Him. Jesus is holy; by perfecting us he guides us to imitate his holiness and consecration to God.

Years after meeting my brother, God gave me the opportunity to live with him for a few months. In that coexistence, I actually got to know him more. Before that, I didn't know his past, I didn't know his personality; only, living circumstances together, we got to know each other, even more.

Do I still need to meet my brother more? I don't know. Likewise, it happens in our relationship with Jesus.

I can have years gathering in a church, and not even know him; intimate with Jesus Christ goes beyond a place. We need to spend with him all day, check that he likes and dislikes, that cheers or upsets him. The Holy Spirit allows us to know Jesus in our daily life. We feel his rebuke or his peace. He reveals to us if something pleases God, or not.

Although the relationship with Jesus is individual, no one can claim to know it in its entirety, there is always something else. Only God knows him completely.

I am not questioning the greater or lesser relationship of each one of us with Jesus Christ. Let's think, do I know Jesus? Am I really from his family? Are we true sons and daughters of God? Jesus was explicit about it, asked and He answered:

—Who is my mother? Who are my brothers? Then he pointed to his disciples and added: Look, these are my mother and my brothers. For everyone who does the will of my Father who is in heaven is my brother and my sister and my mother.

During the earthly life of Jesus Christ thousands of people saw him, but how many knew him? Who were his brothers? He explained it himself, only those who do God's will.

Immersed in a deep crisis in Venezuela, the presence of Jesus Christ in life has been, and is, vital.

By obeying his call I left a transnational company without knowing my future. Months later, I understood, He wanted to make me a writer. I have depended on Him in everything, in money, I knew Him as a provider. In their own way, through others, and bending my pride, I learned to receive before learning to give.

From adultery, I got four herniated discs. Two of them were eliminated with surgery; the others suddenly worsened and left me bedridden. I didn't have health insurance, but I worked for the healing God. One noon, in my heart, I spoke with the Chief (Jesus Christ), minutes later, I received the miracle and walked without difficulty.

A year after getting divorced, between dreams and a deep conviction of his voice in my heart, He explained to me that his will was to reconcile me with my wife. That instruction changed all my plans. Above all, with that case, I met Jesus Christ as Lord. Waiting, trusting, I learned to obey him. I will bring her back —Jesus told me, to the heart.

As an athlete I knew him as my strength. In solitude I met him as my brother. Most men of God are formed in a desert.

In the four Gospels, we have the example of life that Jesus offers us. We need to strive to live in peace with everyone and strive to lead a holy life. Those who are not saints will not see the Lord, says the Bible. We must care for one another, so that none of us will stop receiving the grace of God.

Above all we must protect the heart. We must take care of it; avoid the poisonous root of Satan's deception. Being free from deception, we can help liberate many more Christians.

By giving life to Jesus, we can know him in intimacy. To know Him, we need to trust Him, depend on Him, above all, love Him and obey Him.

In the earthly, our maturity can be measured by the independence of others. When we are children, we depend on our parents, but when we grow up, we don't. For God is different, spiritual maturity is measured by our absolute dependence on Jesus Christ.

To obey it, at the level required by the church, we must know it as the Apostle Paul put it, who wrote to the Philippians: "But how many things were for me gain, I have esteemed as loss for the love of Christ. And certainly, I still esteem all things as a loss for the excellence of the knowledge of Jesus, my Lord, for whose sake I have lost everything, and I have it for garbage, to win Christ. "

We need that level, although it sounds exaggerated.

The church, the true body of Christ, depends on us, its members. To win in the spiritual war we must reach a level of obedience to God, to Jesus, fear of the Lord, convenience and love.

Like not loving Jesus Christ, yes, the only one who justifies us is Jesus with His love, with His grace and with His blood. He is the only guarantee of being holy and healthy. It's our highest manifestation from heaven to earth. Jesus is our only hope of being justified. He is our only chance to be freed from the yoke of evil. He is our ultimate revelation to give, for He gave his life for love.

Christ is the only clear sign we have to demonstrate a change before society. Our peace, despite the circumstances, makes us reflect Jesus from the heart, shine in the darkness. He is the solid and stable rock of all Christians.

Jesus Christ changes lives for good and forever. Christians, if they don't change, they don't know Jesus.

With the preaching of grace without repentance, Satan achieves churches with much appearance but little experience. To know Jesus, implies to look like Jesus. As I read in said "Like father like son". Son of God looks like Jesus, or is not a child of God. Every son resembles something, his father and brother. If

Jesus, my brother, never loses, always wins, then Satan can never win. We ourselves lose when we turn away from God, from the eternal winner, the strongest, sovereign, Jesus Christ.

Jesus came into the world and gives us understanding to know His truth. We are in Him, with Him. He is the truth, true God and eternal life.

Jesus Christ is the good shepherd, he knows his sheep. Who we are his sheep, we know his voice, if we get lost, He always looks for us, loves us.

Let's be God's sheep. Listen to the voice of Jesus, never to Satan. There are Christians suffering in hell. Jesus Christ sought them, they didn't return. He doesn't force anyone; they didn't repent because Satan had taken over their hearts.

Maybe they were not true sheep of Christ?

I dare not say so. The servant of God saw Jesus saddened by seeing these people suffer. Conversing with these souls, He demonstrated how He sought them, but, they themselves decided not to return to God. Jesus Christ doesn't force anyone to return to Him.

The Bible is true. To all his sons and daughters, God always warns us. He loves us. Recall the second letter of the Apostle Peter, who wrote:

"Certainly, if having escaped from the contaminations of the world, through the knowledge of the Lord and Savior Jesus Christ, getting entangled again in them are overcome, their last state becomes worse than the first."

The warning is blunt, he added:

"Because it would have been better for them not to have known the way of justice, that after having known it, to turn back from the holy commandment that was given to them. But the true proverb has happened to them: The dog returns to its vomit, and the sow washed to wallow in the mud. "

Jesus Christ knows the future, knows exactly what is going to happen. For that, he warns us. God wants to forgive us, as long as we repent.

Remember, Peter. Jesus said to him:

—I tell you, the cock will not sing today until you have denied three times that you know me.

Also, remember Judas. Jesus asked him:

— Would you betray the Son of Man with a kiss?

Both disciples betrayed Jesus, Peter denied it and Judas delivered him. Christians, we know it.

What was the difference?

Judas committed suicide, instead, Peter repented.

74

After the resurrection, Jesus asked him:

Pedro, do you love me? Sir, you know everything. You know I love you — Pedro answered. Then, feed my sheep —added Jesus.

Jesus chose Peter to feed his sheep. He assigned a special purpose. He call him, He chose him.

What would have been Peter's eternal destiny if he had not fed the sheep of Jesus? If he had disobeyed, where would Peter be today?

As Christians we want benefits without taking on responsibilities. Every call of God is a special privilege. Being chosen to serve Jesus is an honor. Not fulfilling that purpose is serious.

In this regard, the Apostle Paul always expressed concern to fulfill his call. In the first letter to the Corinthians, he wrote:

Don't you realize that in a race everyone runs, but only one person gets the prize? So run to win! All athletes train with discipline. They do it to win a prize that will fade, but we do it for an eternal prize. That is why I run every step with purpose.

Not only do I hit the air. I discipline my body as an athlete does; I train it to do what it should do. Otherwise, I fear that, after preaching to others, I myself will be disqualified.

As we can read, the apostle Paul knew it. He could be disqualified from the eternal prize. For that reason, he disciplined his body to do what he had to, he struggled with his weaknesses. If he was wrong, he repented, he recognized grace, and he didn't abuse her.

As we know, Paul was one of the greatest examples of repentance. Before converting to Jesus, he persecuted Christians, then, he fought to save them. Every Christian must fight against Satan in the war for his soul, those of his family and many more souls. Before dying, the Apostle Paul wrote:

—As for me, my life was already poured out as an offering to God. The time of my death is approaching. I have fought the good fight, I have finished the race and I have remained faithful. Now the prize awaits me, the crown of justice that the Lord, the just Judge, will give me the day of his return; and the reward is not only for me, but for all who wait with longing for his coming.

Paul met Jesus by revelation, not in person, usually, that is our case. In my case, in three dreams I have seen Jesus, in two dreams I heard his voice, once I saw him in the spirit.

However, I don't know him from those experiences. Whether it's a lot or a little, I met Jesus by obeying him. Therefore, the Apostle John in his first letter explained:

We can be sure that we know God if we obey his commandments. If someone says, "I know God — but he doesn't obey the commandments of God, he is a liar and does not live in the truth; but those who obey the word of God truly demonstrate how much they love Him. This is how we know we live in it. Those who say that they live in God must live as Jesus lived.

Obey Jesus Christ

Knowing Jesus Christ is not enough. Obeying Jesus Christ implies knowing him for real, in intimacy.

If I obey Jesus, I obey God the Father.

Satan always tries to deceive us; his traps always pretend to make us disobey God.

As I mentioned in previous chapters, in Christians, Satan first tries to disable us, seeks to impede our purpose; if he can't, it seeks to kill us; if he doesn't succeed either, he aims at damaging our heart; and if all this fails, he can even try, subtly, to negotiate with us.

Satan knows that if he takes a believer away from his call, he can lead him to lose his salvation. Their deceptions, in general, are desirable things, offers that sound good and look good; like don't look sinful and make us feel fulfilled. If we are not firm in the word of God, we can fall.

Among many examples available in my life, this time I will share with you a warning that God showed me, in the world of sports. As an athlete, in recent years I have investigated this sector of society. Among evident sins, including worshiping Satan, self—centeredness and vainglory predominate in many hearts of athletes.

To those who don't know me, I tell them. One night, in a dream I heard the voice of Jesus, who told me:

—I'm your lord, I have another plan.

Immediately, I saw myself running, even winning.

During my youth I practiced swimming, all my life I thought about dedicating myself to that sport once retired. I never thought about running, I don't like it. I never imagined that God wanted to use me in athletics, nor did I suspect that he would exalt the name of Jesus in sports.

Upon awakening from that dream, I said to Jesus:

— Sir, I don't like to run.

It's easy to do only what we like, Luis, you think I enjoyed dying on a cross — he answered.

Immediately, I remembered the following account of the life of Jesus, moments before surrendering:

Jesus stepped forward a little more and bowed his face to the ground as he prayed: My Father! If possible, let this cup filled with suffering pass from me. However, I want your will to be done, not mine.

Jesus previously knew that suffering, but he didn't avoid it. He had a purpose assigned by God that he had to fulfill it, above his will.

So, similar when Jesus Christ called me to run, although I still don't like it, I also do it.

In that dream I heard:

—I am your Lord, I have another plan.

With "I am your Lord" I recognized that it was Jesus, with "another plan", I assumed that I would continue to fulfill the previous plans that He had assigned me.

After giving my life to God, that is to say, after the day when I told him that I would work for Him, but, that I would prevent my son from disappearing, one night praying, I reaffirmed to Jesus Christ my surrender. Without thinking much, with a sincere heart, I said:

— If I'm going to work for you, Lord, use me then.

That same night, perhaps due to the lightness of my request, God granted me the following dream:

I saw myself alone, in an unknown place. Suddenly a man stood in front of me, pulled out a gun and fired all the bullets. I didn't even have time to move, but, none of the bullets touched me.

When I woke up, anguished, I heard the voice of God in my heart. Between love and firmness, he asked me:

—Are you sure? Do you want me to use you?

That time, I didn't respond so quickly, it took me a few seconds; I thought and, suddenly, I analyzed. If in that dream, no bullet touched me, why fear?

Yes, use me —I answered, as if signing a contract.

In his first plan, Jesus made me a writer. In another plan, I understood his desire to reconcile with my wife; running appeared as an additional plan.

Saving all the differences; like Jesus Christ, being in the form of a man, he humbled himself, becoming obedient to death, and death on a cross; thus, I have to die, daily, to crucify my will, trying to obey him in everything.

If in Jesus Christ we find the perfect model of obedience to God, then how not to obey it.

Obedience to Jesus goes beyond loving him and obeying his commandments, that are indispensable, not enough, daily, we must obey him in everything.

Obeying Jesus Christ is an act of worship, as the Apostle Paul explained to the Romans:

"Therefore, beloved brethren, I beg you to surrender your body to God for all that he has done for you.

May it be a living and holy sacrifice, the kind of sacrifice that pleases him; that is the true way of worshiping him."

In my case, that requirement was and still is literal. From the sedentary lifestyle I had, before the age of 40, I went on to train up to six days a week with one or two sessions a day. As an athlete, I must give my body to God to be molded according to his plan as a runner. Of weighing, almost 100 kilograms, I lowered to 58kg (128 pounds), before, finally stabilize me around 70 kg (154 pounds).

I didn't know those details when I heard "I have another plan". Likewise, when Jesus Christ formed me as a writer, I also didn't know that almost all of our books would be based on testimonies, real events based on circumstances in my life; much less did I suspect that Jesus wanted to use me to teach a lifestyle pleasing to God.

In obeying that order to wait for my wife, I didn't know the details about a family restoration ministry for us either.

When I started running, I didn't know that a brand of sportswear would be associated with my task.

That is, a dear reader, with Jesus Christ obedience works in the following way:

"I obey, therefore I understand."

All those plans are still in process. I believe that I will execute them until the end of my life. Thus, it was the contract signed with the Chief, until the last day.

When asked by the disciples about when certain things would happen, Jesus answered:

—Only the Father has the authority to set those dates and times, and it's not for you to know.

It's that simple. From my own experience I know. In his absolute sovereignty God decides, or not, to say when.

It's not because God doesn't know it, He knows everything and his times are perfect. For example, in a dream I saw how, despite the opposition of his mother, God would bring my son to visit me on Monday. So it happened, exactly on Monday I shared with the kid.

In general, the calls of God are tasks of resistance, not speed. When He call us at His service we need, first, to be trained for battle, because, every service will have opposition. In that preparation comes the desert, difficult circumstances, and necessary tests to form our character. Forty days, forty years, depends on us. If we learn quickly; before we leave the desert. Without the proper character, we see men and women of God, to whom the public placed them, and the public manipulates them. They don't fulfill God's call.

That is why the apostle Paul recognized the need for character, he knew it. To the Romans he wrote:

—We are also happy to face trials and difficulties because we know that they help us to develop resistance. And resistance develops firmness of character, and character strengthens our sure hope of salvation. That hope will not end in disappointment. For we know with what tenderness God loves us who has given us the Holy Spirit to fill our hearts with his love.

Every call implies difficulty. Evil is always opposed. If it flows easily, we need to verify who we are obeying: to Jesus or to Satan?

Returning to the example of sport, I share with you, two other dreams, where I was warned.

In the first, I was locked in a mansion. With me there were three athletes closest to me. The owner of the mansion, who was a tall man with bright blond hair and cold eyes, called us. One of the athletes had red eyes, he only followed that man's instructions, his weakness was the longing for fame. I saw that accepting a sponsorship could take it away from its purpose. Another was sitting at a table eating delicacies, the gluttony could dominate him. A baseball player, was imprisoned in the house, his mother shouted from the outside asking the man to release his son but he answered "no". I saw myself in the basement, surrounded by beautiful women.

As always, when I woke up, I asked God if that was his dream. Praying, I understood. The blond man was Satan. It was a warning from Jesus. The four of us would be tempted according to our sinful roots. In what I saw, I understood the weak points.

I warned the three athletes, and I took care of myself. One of the athletes accepted the patronage that God warned us, from there, he began to move away from his pleasant lifestyle before God. The longing for fame clouded his spiritual vision. At his discretion because he calls Jesus Lord, he thinks he's obeying Him. Because he feels peace, he believes he is right with God. He doesn't feel the rebuke in his spirit, because, although he grew up in the gospel, and knows the word, he has not received the Holy Spirit.

Without the Holy Spirit of God, Satan deceives anyone. From the Gospel of Luke: "So if you, sinful people, know how to give good gifts to your children, how much more will your heavenly Father give the Holy Spirit to those who ask for it." If you have not yet received the Holy Spirit, then ask God for it.

In the second dream, which I saw months after the first one, I saw again the athlete who gave in to his longing for fame, this time we saw ourselves in an Olympic village. The other two athletes didn't appear that time. Known only I saw my friend and his brother, the rest were unknown people. In that dream, Jesus Christ allowed me to see the main sins within the athletes in Venezuela, but, whatever the continent, sins are similar. I walked through areas of homosexuality, witchcraft, vainglory (where my friend was), fornication (I saw myself following an ex—girlfriend). I just was not allowed to enter a place called the "new circus", in which, I understood, there were athletes who sold their souls to Satan in exchange for their success as athletes. I saw those places desperate, trying to escape. He didn't belong there, he knew, he could not find the way out.

When I woke up again, I felt the voice of Jesus with a warning in my heart. The devil wants our heads and will seek to deceive us to get us out of the purpose within the sport. In my case, I once heard an apostle who explained how every man of God must deal with one or several women used to try to deceive him.

I fight with the temptation before women who can represent an excellent alternative for my life. Our peace cannot depend on anything or anyone. Jesus filled my heart to teach me to have peace only, and then, to remain in peace accompanied.

Several years ago, it was when Jesus showed me that I had to reconcile with my wife. One night, I asked God to make her happy with her partner. Suddenly, firmly, in my heart, He told me:

—Don't ask that. That is not my will; I don't have to bless a relationship based on adultery.

Until that moment, I didn't know God's firmness regarding adultery and divorce. Although I have committed adultery, and perhaps she too, at least in her heart, that doesn't allow us to rebuild our lives with someone, without being in sin. Before God, any relationship outside of marriage is adultery.

That same year, I decided to spend a vacation with a beautiful model. Although, I already knew that God wanted to reconcile me, in my arguments I didn't see badly having a temporary relationship while waiting for reconciliation with my wife. The first night, a reproach rose in me, on the way to the room I lost my peace, so much so, that upon entering, I asked God:

—If this doesn't suit me, please, when I put my head on the pillow, put me down to sleep immediately.

And so it happened.

That night I dreamed about my wife, who told me:

—As well as I help you with your ministry and mission.

There, I didn't understand those words. When Jesus showed me the purpose with my wife, I remembered them.

The second night, while the beautiful model bathed, I reflected: "She is an excellent alternative to rebuild my life." Convinced, I said to God:

—Open our hearts; let us be her and me.

Luis, if you want I'll do it, are you sure? That is not my will — answered God in my heart.

I am not saying that God is a kind of genius of the lamp that grants our capricious desires, but, I heard that in my heart.

Immediately, I remembered Jesus, I answered like Him:

— Don't! Father, your will be done and not mine.

Months later I saw the lady. I understood how God protected me; He saved me from losing my call. The Holy Spirit guided me to make that decision, because, by my human strength, it would have been impossible.

When Jesus Christ showed me his family plan to reconcile me with my wife, from the beginning he said:

—Don't do anything, this doesn't depend on you, it's up to me, I'll bring her back when you're ready.

Years passed, God announced to me that my wife would have a daughter with her partner, and it happened. However, during her pregnancy, in a dream I saw that girl die before being born. It will happen right at the end because of lack of nutrients — Jesus said in the dream.

He didn't say that God would kill her, but she would die. When the time came, the girl was born. Before the dream, when asked. Jesus Christ answered me, to the heart:

"Every time you see that girl, you will remember my mercy. I always have the last word.

It has not been easy to wait several years for my wife's return. Many times I have been tempted to escape my purpose. At first, I was tempted to leave the country. Professionally I had opportunities in other places, but God wants to keep me in Venezuela for several more years. Then, I will live a few years out, but, always keeping my home in this country. My purpose, despite being international, is based in Valencia as a center of operations.

The greatest temptations to stop waiting for reconciliation with my wife have always happened through women, even within the church.

In a moment, let's say of wear and tear in front of so many months of waiting, in the church where I gather I saw a beautiful lady. The attraction was unusual and always coincided with her. As God knows all my thoughts, one night, unable to get it out of my mind, I began to pray for explanations.

She is the greatest temptation you have to disobey me — answered God in my heart.

Praying, I understood. Although the lady is Christian, she has a purpose different from mine. Also, I am legally divorced, but married before God.

Do you accept her as a wife? — Said a priest, one night, years ago— in health and disease, in wealth and poverty, until death do you part?

Yes, I do —I replied, drunk.

Then I declare them, husband and wife —he added.

Neither adultery, nor fornication, nor getting drunk, is a valid argument before God to break the sacred covenant I made with Him, one night in a church. God unites purposes. The only help suitable for my purpose is my wife. Since before our birth, we were chosen to fulfill their plans. As a family, our success will be measured by the fruits of our children, by their works before God. Our obedience blesses other people, just as disobedience negatively affects others. Not only ourselves, we all influence other lives for better or worse. I began to obey God out of fear, to the death of my son, mainly. With the advance of the call, I learned to obey him out of fear of the Lord. Then, out of fear and convenience. Currently, I am trying to obey him out of love.

First level: Obedience out of fear

Satan's deception in the preaching of grace without repentance is so subtle that it guides men and women of God to do their own will over the plans and purpose of Jesus Christ.

It's indispensable to understand, never forget, when we receive Jesus in our life we become his brothers, heirs of the great King. As members of His family we have responsibilities. We protect our people, we fight for their souls.

Satan's fight against God is for people. The devil wants to steal, kill and destroy the most precious creation of God, that is, the human being. Every Christian who loses his salvation, dying, ends up in hell, any sinner, unconverted. Maybe it doesn't end in the lake of fire, but in the outer darkness. Be one or another place, suffering is eternal.

Spiritual warfare for the eternal destiny of souls has only two sides, good and evil. Who is not with me is against me —said Jesus. In that battle, trying to remain neutral is even worse. The warning is obvious. Remember the following verse of the Bible: I know everything you do, that you are neither cold nor hot. How I wish you were the one or the other! But since you are warm, neither cold nor hot, I will spit you out of my mouth! —Said God.

If someone, Christian or not, today is not serving God; consequently, he is serving Satan.

Free will allows us to choose life and truth, to follow Jesus Christ who sets us free. Every Christian believes that he follows him, but does our life please God? Are we doing his will?

With that question I go beyond the issue of living outside of sin, fulfilling God's commands. The will of Jesus Christ goes above that. It's to fulfill the eternal purpose for which we have been called, the particular contribution that God assigns us as part of his team, inside and outside the church.

Every war is won with strategy, tactics and operations. In spiritual war the only general of good is God the Father, He is the one who establishes the strategy. Jesus Christ in permanent agreement with Him is the one who leads the tactics assigned to each one of the Christians; and we are the ones in charge of the operations, always guided by the Holy Spirit.

If we disobey our call, we risk both the life of our earthly family and the lives of other members of God's family. The obvious disobedience of every Christian is "not to heed the call of Jesus," that particular task to which God can call each one of his children. If we attend to the "call", the next disobedience may be "half obedience". That is, start to fulfill the call, and then escape.

In that situation, there are those who obey God for a time, they advance in their call, but, then they don't continue with it for whatever reason. That is something dangerous in the life of every Christian, outside the will of Jesus (conscious or unconscious) we can be outside his protection. If we leave the will without realizing it, then the Holy Spirit guides us to react, but if we ignore his voice, it can be serious. From my own experience, I know.

Beginning to fulfill my call, I made much more mistakes than I think I am making now. I am still alive because I have asked for forgiveness and I have repented when I have moved away from the will of God. I always suffered consequences; sin opens a gap, small or large, in the spiritual world.

In addition to half obeying or disobeying the call, there is another serious case of disobedience. That is "obedience according to my own opinion".

For example, a person receives the pastoral call and advances by preparing. One day God decides to choose him, that is, he proceeds to raise him as Pastor.

In his strategy, God informs him: You must open a church in city A, on street 1. When does disobedience by obedience occur according to my own opinion: When that Pastor decided in his own opinion to open the church on the 2nd street or even further away, in the city B. Sometimes we believe we know more than God, we decide and not He.

If God, the All-Knowing, who knows all, commanded to open that church city A 1 street is, first, because it's possible; second, because he has a specific plan on the site; third, because the true sheep of the Shepherd could, just, get to that place.

That is an example, but obedience in our own opinion can be subtly rooted in us, servants and servants of the Lord Jesus Christ.

Other examples, songs with different letters to those revealed, sometimes to make them more popular. You preach with modified messages, from developers to motivators. Books with plots oriented to more readers. Obvious cases or subtly disguised.

From my own experience, I verified how I can use the gift of a writer to write for God or for the devil. Blessing or curse, it depends on me.

After my first book, God sent me to train as a writer in an academy.

In one of the subjects, I took the opportunity and wrote a story to a beautiful young woman. A relative was sick, she expected a miracle. My intention was not to help her, but to make her fall in love. Newly converted, spiritual baby, I used the gift and created an excellent story. The young woman, delighted, enjoyed seeing herself on the cover, other readers congratulated me, I myself recognized the quality of that work. From the literary point of view, it was excellent.

However, months later I felt something wrong in my life, praying, I discovered it. I opened that story, I read it completely and verified how I described a miracle, without mentioning Jesus, in any part of the story. I changed the plot of the story to take it from something real; her niece had miraculously saved herself, to write a love story between the girl and me.

I think that God was merciful to me in that error, given my spiritual immaturity. At that time I didn't know the reconciliation plan with my wife either. However, with discernment, one night I burned that story, I couldn't afford to leave open any gap in the spiritual world.

While reading this testimony, someone may think there was nothing wrong, but if I had it, God gave me a gift to use it for Jesus Christ, if I write for myself, it's idolatry to myself, which is serious. Another may think why some versions of their books use their photos as covers? Because they are testimonies based on real events in my life and I have felt the direction of using those photos.

From successes and mistakes, in several years of service, I learned to seek the will of God. I started, obeying Jesus Christ for fear of the consequences of disobeying him. That night, when I saw my desperate wife with the posters of "missing child", panic seized me, only after offering my life to God, by deciding to work for Jesus Christ, and telling him, did I manage to feel peace.

From the first moment, Jesus Christ revealed himself to me as my Chief, I confess. I respect it as such. Someone may think "that dream of the missing child was not from God" because I couldn't afford to prove it. In my heart I received it as a warning, and I will always be grateful to warn me. Other dreams have been fulfilled, pleasant and unpleasant, Jesus warned me, my son was saved, I owe my life to him until the end.

As in a company, at first I didn't know my boss. Sometimes I obeyed him for fear of punishment, sometimes for fear of being fired. It was not fear.

As I got to know him I understood his love. His plan was to use my son as a tool to save me.

With the call I understood the love of God and the privileged place where we are his chosen ones. Many are called but few are chosen, we can read it in the Gospel according to Matthew.

In my case, forty months elapsed from God's call as a writer, until he was elected to a teaching ministry. From being called to being elected, I passed tests. Jesus Christ, first, calls us, if we pass the tests, he chooses us.

During that period I obeyed the Chief, Jesus Christ, out of fear, then that fear turned into fear. A holy fear that can be explained as something between respect and love for God the Father, God the Son and God the Holy Spirit.

The fear of the Lord is true wisdom.

That revealing statement we can read in the Bible, in Proverbs, King Solomon wrote.

This fear of the Lord is different from fear.

Similarly, to earthly life, when we are children, we obey parents out of respect. Those who obey out of fear don't have a healthy relationship with their parents. The same happens in our spiritual life; If we are afraid of God, our Father, then, we don't know him in intimacy.

Don't fear Satan; fear God —said Jesus.

The fear is not of Christians. The Holy Spirit never gives us a spirit of cowardice. On the contrary, He always gives us power, love and self—control. Without the Holy Spirit we are easily defeated by Satan. That is why Jesus received the Holy Spirit before facing Satan in the desert. We need the Holy Spirit, even more than Jesus.

The fear of the Lord, that is necessary in life. All disobedience to God leads to sin, and sin leads to death. The disobedience of the first man, Adam, initiated sin and spiritual death, from there, we lost intimacy with God.

Who lives without God is spiritually dead. Without Jesus Christ, we are spiritually dead. Likewise, we need to receive the Holy Spirit.

The obedience of Jesus Christ restored our entire communion with God; we can have intimacy with God, because we believe in Jesus. The disobedience of Adam made us sinners, Jesus makes us righteous.

Knowing Jesus Christ implies obeying him.

Only through obedience to God do we enjoy his earthly blessings and eternal life. In Jesus Christ, we are vivified, we depend on Him, and we must know Him in everything and obey Him in everything.

In my case, in dreams and visions, I receive part of the information necessary to fulfill my call. In revelations, I see the plans, or I receive warnings.

Eternal life depends on believing in the resurrection of Jesus Christ and making him the Lord of our life.

Salvation is never a reward for works. Every Christian knows that, perfectly. Salvation is an undeserved gift; therefore, we must take care of it.

The preaching of grace without repentance has deceived millions of people, who, not feeling sorry, are considered "good". If they don't commit obvious sins, they are considered righteous. They neglect salvation; they believe they will reach heaven without a true Lordship of Jesus in their lives.

I share with you two cases, in which I was involved, a couple of lessons related to heaven and hell, one I wanted to see, but the other did not.

Years ago, being a Christian already and obeying the call, on vacation, I traveled to my hometown; with my father, where his aunt lived, an old woman of about ninety years of age. Surprised at his longevity, I asked myself, is she still alive because she hasn't received Jesus? Could it be that God is still looking to save her?

One night, I went into her room and asked:

—Aunt, do you want to receive Jesus Christ in your heart?

Yes, what should I do? —She said, smiling.

Repeat this prayer with me, if you open your heart to God and pray with sincerity, you will receive it. Then, I said: — "Lord JESUS, today I open my heart to receive you, I recognize that I have disobeyed you, I have lived away from you and I repent, I apologize for all my sins. I give myself to you; I give you my anxieties, problems, needs, fears, resentments and plans. I recognize you as my only and sufficient Savior. Please write my name in the book of life, fulfill your purpose in me, and teach me the way, the truth and the life that you are. Your kingdom come to me. Amen".

Dear reader, something similar I prayed one day. Thus, I received Jesus and my whole life changed for good and forever. Today you have that opportunity. If you are not yet a Christian, if you have not yet received Christ in your heart, today is the day to receive it. Read that prayer aloud, be it alone or accompanied, read it aloud, with a sincere heart, and believe you will receive it.

That night, the aunt received Jesus in her heart.

The following year, I returned on vacation to my father's house. In my heart I had the case of the aunt. When I arrived, I went to her room to greet her, I asked her:

—Aunt, how is you with Jesus Christ?

Jesus is here in my heart — she answered, smiling, giving herself a gentle blow on her chest.

In that moment, I felt peace for her life. With me, I was a Christian friend, immediately, I said:

—We win this soul for Jesus Christ.

After a few months, suddenly, one Saturday I felt the undoubted instruction in my heart, Jesus sent me to my father's house, immediately.

The next day, on Sunday, I again traveled to my hometown, but, this time, driving totally alone. On the tour, I prayed several hours in the spirit. Suddenly, praying, I understood the reason for my trip.

Aunt will die —I heard in my heart.

She was sick, but it could last month's like that. When I arrived, after dinner, on Sunday night, I informed my father, without knowing, when it would happen.

Before going to sleep, my son came to her aunt's room because he heard her complain. He saw it for a second and, immediately, we went to bed.

When I prayed, before going to sleep, my son said:

—God, please, don't let my aunt suffer.

The next afternoon, Monday, the aunt died.

The first to find out was me. I entered to see her, but she wasn't breathing, I looked for her pulse and she didn't have any. Her body was still hot. Dead, I would have a few minutes.

I felt peace, I believed and I trusted in his eternal destiny, two years before, I had won that soul for Jesus.

However, I asked God to confirm if the aunt was in heaven. I didn't tell anyone, but I begged a revealing dream, I wanted confirmation.

After several nights, of that, I had no dream. Suddenly, one night, talking on the phone with my father's wife, she told me:

—Luis, last night I dreamed of my aunt, I was young, happy, walking in a beautiful place, she looked at me and greeted me.

Upon hearing that dream, I felt the confirmation in my heart, the aunt is saved. Perhaps, God did not give me the dream because I could think that I had imagined it, because I wanted it. He confirmed that salvation through a dream of another person.

That experience awakened in me a greater longing for the salvation of people; out of any possible reward. For that, I was called and elected.

Heaven and hell, they are real. The aunt is in heaven, but not all souls have that same destiny.

Weeks after the death of the aunt, my father told me that his mother, my grandmother, was sick.

Dad, the only problem is not that she's sick, but the serious thing is that she could die without Jesus Christ in her heart, the greatest suffering is in hell —I said.

A few days later, she got worse. Suddenly, one afternoon, I received the message from my father, the grandmother died.

In my heart I felt her eternal destiny. I remembered how good it was with everyone; but, I cried thinking about her soul. Suddenly, I stopped crying, I managed to speak, and I shouted:

—God, why didn't you send me to tell my grandmother about Jesus Christ?

At that time, my grandmother was in the same street where my son lived. There was that excuse to go see her and tell her about Jesus. God was able to send me to see my son and visit my grandmother. In my pain, Satan attacked my heart. God didn't want to save her, the devil repeated in my mind. Suddenly, I screamed and looked at the sky.

Many spoke to her about Jesus —I heard in my soul.

My suffering for the grandmother, passed to resignation. God was aware and his decision was already made.

I don't want to see her eternal destiny —I asked God.

Although I asked not to see her, in a dream I saw my grandmother, in ashes, suffering, I verified her eternal destiny. Likewise, I saw my grandfather, suffering in hell.

As I saw them in different places and sufferings, I inquired about it. My grandmother is in the outer darkness; my grandfather, in the lake of fire.

Jesus mentioned both places, we can read it in the Gospels Mark, Matthew and Luke. In hell, the servant of God saw more of those places.

Despite being together until the end of their lives, the reasons for going to hell were different between my grandfather and my grandmother. My grandfather, led an unpleasant life in the eyes of God before his old age, never repented, and even opened evil doors taking it as games. I remember how, sometimes, when he drank, he would be quiet playing domino, and then he would say that the "Negro Felipe" was talking to him. I don't know if any entity of evil spoke to him or not, but, jokingly or seriously, my grandfather opened doors to Satan until he lost his soul. That is why it ended in a place of suffering different from my grandmother.

The case of my grandmother, resounded in my mind, but, confirmed what was warned in the Bible. It's not by works; it's by faith in Jesus Christ. My grandmother all her life was a good person (in my opinion), I never saw her doing something wrong, nor did I hear her saying bad words, she fell into the deception of Satan to adore, to follow virgins and saints. Jesus was not his only Lord and Savior. That's why it ended up in the outer darkness.

The Virgin Mary was an example of obedience, a true servant of God, someone to whom we owe respect, honor, never adoration, Mary was a human being more. I do not know if she died or was taken to heaven; I do not know either, if he had children after Jesus. Any worship of dead humans is idolatry. We must worship God, Jesus Christ and the Holy Spirit. Millions believe that Jesus was resurrected and is the Son of God, but fall into that deception of Satan, adore virgins and saints. Upon hearing that truth, they justify that they don't adore them but revere them. The theme of praying to virgins and saints is a hoax. The only intercessor between God and humans is Jesus Christ.

In Catholic churches, although Jesus Christ is the center, the exaltation of virgins and saints diverts the attention of believers. Intimacy with Jesus doesn't depend on speaking to a plaster figure, not even because that figure represents Jesus Christ. In Christian churches when the pastor is the protagonist, he diverts believers from intimacy with Jesus. We can all be saints in the eyes of God; we just need to obey all his will with Jesus Christ as our only Lord and Savior. If we only do a part of God's will, without wanting to it, we can be displeasing God in something. The will of God is always good, pleasant and perfect. Obedience to God matures. First, I obeyed Jesus out of fear of the Lord. Then, one day, I began to obey Jesus for convenience.

Second level: Obedience out of convenience

As they tell me, my grandmother received a miracle and attributed it to José Gregorio Hernández, a former doctor whom many Venezuelans attribute healing; that idolatry, inherited by some daughters and grandchildren. Even a cousin of mine claims to have seen Dr. Hernandez. Satan disguises himself as an angel of light, the apostle Paul warned the Corinthians.

An evil spirit could be responsible for my grandmother's illness. If so, Satan could have taken out that spirit of illness, and then deceived it. According to the story, that doctor Hernandez was someone remarkable.

Probably, he was saved, and he is in heaven; but, that doctor or any other saved person who is in heaven, does miracles of healing or anything. These are Satan's deceptions to drive believers away from Jesus Christ, guiding them to hell.

Now, God told me: Many people told him about Jesus. The miracle of my grandmother could be of Jesus. In the church she heard about Jesus, many told her about him, but she didn't know Jesus, he was not her Lord. Without liberation, every sinful root remains in families for generations.

My grandmother's idolatry, my grandfather's fornication, perhaps inherited, I don't know. From my father, the curse of divorce began.

Our future depends on obeying Jesus. By Jesus, we can be free from every curse. Just as I, for his eternal well-being, my father must give his life to Jesus Christ and my son as well. The future of others depends on the obedience of the three. Abraham and his descendants were blessed, from their obedience. All of us, we have the opportunity to receive the blessings of God; we just have to obey it. Remember, the episode.

"Take your son, your only son Isaac, whom you love, and go to the land of Moriah. Offer him there as a burnt offering on one of the mountains I will show you." —said God.

When they arrived at the place indicated by God, Abraham built an altar and placed the wood on top. Then he bound his son Isaac, and put him on the altar, on top of the wood. Abraham took the knife to kill his son in sacrifice. At that moment, the angel of the Lord, from heaven, called him:

—Abraham! Abraham!

"Yes" — said Abraham — "here I am!"

— Don't lay your hand on the boy or do anything to him, for now I know that you fear God, seeing you have not withheld your son, your only son, from me.

One day, I gave my son to God, for the good of both. Your purpose is a big burden for me.

God made a promise to Abraham, he would have a son, he waited many years until he had that baby. Later, God asked for his son in sacrifice. We must obey without understanding. I obey, therefore I understand.

Abraham obeyed because of fear of the Lord, without any benefit. My friend Abraham —said God. We can read it in Isaiah. Obedience made him a friend of God.

Our obedience to God through Jesus allows us to achieve the necessary intimacy until we are considered his friends. God always seeks us, besides Father, He longs to be our friend.

In my case, after three years of marriage, a marital crisis occurred. By the mercy of God, at that time, we didn't get to divorce. Overcoming contraceptive methods, my wife got pregnant. From the temporary reconciliation, to the sexual relationship, until overcoming the obstacles, God configured a plan to bring our son to the world.

Without knowing my purpose, I thought that a son would give meaning to my existence. Today, I love my son with all my heart, but, I felt the real reason to live when I discovered my call to serve God through Jesus. In adolescence, I had thoughts of suicide. Now, I crave eternal life.

With the pregnancy, we both saw a divine sign to continue together. Among passing joys, our relationship was never solid. When Satan, with fury, attacks a marriage, it's impossible to save it without Jesus.

Even having a child, our relationship didn't improve. Far from God, in my analysis, I looked for a solution to save my marriage. My wife rejected me, I was unbearable. I planned to have a lover.

I talked with my lady friends, none of them supported me, in each talk, they all said:

—Don't do it, you're going to destroy your family.

I met my lover on a plane. Satan took control of me and I even put her to work with me.

One day, my wife asked me to separate. Without my knowing it, she knew about my lover, that was not her argument. For my son, I refused to leave my house.

The next week, the company sent me to work in another city. In my loneliness at the hotel, one dawn I started to cry, I knelt down and said:

—God, tell me what to do, the best for all three.

Separate — I heard God in my heart.

As I asked, and he answered, I felt conviction. I returned to my house, I agreed to the separation, but, my mistake was to talk about "divorce". There, I opened the spiritual gap.

God sent me to separate, not divorce.

In the Bible, that recommendation is mentioned in marriages, as long as the separated time serves in both to seek intimacy with God.

To move out, I demanded a legal separation agreement from my wife. Without reconciliation, in a year, we had to divorce. In those months, a fight between good and evil was fought in my heart. When my father left my house, peace reigned; the arguments with my mother were bad. That peace was brought by Satan to my mind, and I began to live with my lover. At first, it was heaven; then, it was hell in life. Cast my lover out of the apartment, it cost money. To leave me, she asked for an exact amount of money. She threatened to demonstrate workplace harassment. She became the victim.

My worst crisis began when leaving my house. Four herniated discs, traffic accident, among others.

When I wanted a young lover, God allowed it. In wanting women of one night, he also allowed it. Although God allowed it that was never his will. He always had control of my life, my mistakes weren't worse because Jesus protected me.

If the accident didn't happen, the woman who drove would have become pregnant. In prayer, I understood it. God always had control, He only allowed mistakes later. It prevented me from falling into homosexuality, witchcraft, other sins, and even crimes, apart from those useful in my current testimonies. When Jesus calls us to his service, He knows our past.

Reconciling me with my wife will be a useful testimony for millions of people, God could prevent it, but, he took advantage of our mistake to use us in that. At first, I obeyed because of fear of the Lord. Then, God began to show me, in dreams, his plan for my whole family. I have seen the purpose of my wife, my son's call, and many more revelations about our individual, family future. Good plans.

Remember, the biblical verse where it says:

—God is not a man, He does not lie. He is not human; He does not change His mind. Did He ever speak without acting? Have He ever promised without fulfilling?

In addition to obeying God for fear of the Lord, I decided to hold on to his promises and obey God, also, our convenience. Salvation is, without a doubt, the main promise of God. Thus, like that, every promise deserves obedience to receive it; we must take care of every promise, because we can lose them.

Some may disagree with me. Remember, the people of Israel who left Egypt was not the same to reach the Promised Land. Almost all the people of Israel, except Joshua and Caleb, disobeyed God and perished in the desert. The trip, it should last forty days, but, it became forty years. Moreover, not even Moses stepped on the Promised Land; he died, before reaching it.

Through disobedience, any of us can lose the promises. Also, we can delay them for disobedient, and, may receive one of the following generations. Out of convenience, we must focus on receiving the full reward.

In the first letter of the apostle John, we read:

—Be careful not to lose what we have achieved with so much work. Be diligent to receive a full reward.

If the apostle mentioned a complete reward it is because, there is also an incomplete reward.

In this case, we talk about something beyond salvation. Those of us who enjoy eternal well—being have assured rewards. While that happens, we have blessings, health, money, love and many other things that God has planned for those who love him.

Therefore, we need to work willingly always, in everything, as for the Lord Jesus Christ; Not like anyone in this world, aware that God will reward us. If we obey, we keep his covenant; we are a special treasure among the nations. The whole earth belongs to Him. Remember, this:

Blessed are those who hear the word of God and put it into practice —Jesus taught. Faith without works is dead, explained the apostle James.

We cannot just listen to the word of God. We must put it into practice; otherwise, we are deceiving ourselves. That is serious. If we listen to the word and don't obey, it's like seeing ourselves in a mirror. We see ourselves; we move away and forget how we are.

If we observe, carefully, the perfect law that liberates us, the Bible. If we do what is written in it, and we don't forget what we hear from it, God blesses us for doing his will.

If someone says, "I know God", but doesn't obey God's commandments, that person is a liar and is not living in the truth. But, those who always obey the word of God, truly, show how completely they love Him. This is how we know that we live in Him. Those who say that they live in God must live their lives as Jesus did —the Apostle John explained in his first letter.

There is no other alternative; our model of life is the example of Jesus. Pastors, apostles, teachers, men and women of God can guide us, but, the true pattern to follow is Jesus Christ.

Our obedience to God always demonstrates faith.

When God showed me the reconciliation with my wife, He emphasized: it depends on me; I will bring it when you are ready, and you must not fail again. She has not returned and more than forty months have passed since that order. In obedience to God, I should not have any approach to it outside of the direction of Jesus Christ. However, believing that this will happen, I continue to prepare for his return, physically, spiritually, morally, even in an altered way. From the soul, thoughts and emotions come, without self-control a man of God can fail.

All that preparation involves visible and invisible changes. Among God's wishes, I saw the body He wants for me, to fulfill His purpose as an athlete, and even for my wife's enjoyment.

Our obedience is the best sacrifice.

Recall the case of Saul, the reason why God rejected him. "I regret to have made Saul king, because he has not been loyal to me and he has refused to obey my command" — the Lord told Samuel.

Then, the prophet Samuel told King Saul:

—Why did you not obey the Lord? Why did you hurry to take the spoils and do what is bad in the eyes of the Lord?

"Go and completely destroy the sinners —the Amalekites— until all are dead." That had been God's order, to Saul.

But I did obey the Lord! — Said Sau —. I fulfilled the mission he entrusted to me! I brought King Agag, but I destroyed all the others.

Dear reader, not obeying absolutely the whole order of God, is serious. He ordered him to destroy "all" but Saul decided to leave "one" alive. That episode of Saul serves as an example. We can believe that we obeyed God, when, perhaps, something was missing, insignificant for us, important for God. Incomplete obedience, it's disobedience before God.

Continuing the case of King Saul; next, Samuel replied:

—What is the most pleasing to the Lord: your burnt offerings and sacrifices, or that you obey his voice? Listen out! Obedience is better than sacrifice, and submission is better than offering the fat of rams. Rebellion is as sinful as sorcery and stubbornness, as bad as worshiping idols. So, because you have rejected the Lord's command, he has rejected you as king.

Finally, Samuel said:

Bring me King Agag, whom Saul did not kill.

Agag arrived full of hope, because he thought: «Surely the worst has already happened, and I have been freed from death! ».

It was not so. Samuel killed him before the Lord.

Brother, sister, you who read these lines, if the person chosen for a task doesn't fulfill it, then, God chooses another to do it. The divine purpose always prevails, above any human.

Nobody is indispensable. If Jesus Christ calls us to serve him, we should obey him. He waits a while, if we don't, he chooses another one, that simple. For fear of the Lord and out of convenience, Saul had to obey in everything, he was King. Let us learn from the case, once rejected, God put David as King.

Third level: Obedience out of love

The next lines were written, even for me. I recognize the highest level of obedience as obedience out of love. However, I don't dare to believe, even, that I have reached that level. Therefore, let's read; let's learn from the example of Jesus.

God so loved the world that he gave his only Son, so that everyone who believes in him will not be lost, but will have eternal life —Jesus taught.

Abraham was tested, but in the end he didn't sacrifice his son. On the other hand, God did give his to all of us. The one who has children knows the magnitude of the pain when seeing one of their own suffers, imagine for a moment, seeing a son die, being innocent, in cruel and announced death. Thus, God saw Jesus.

God feels, He loves, He suffers, He rejoices. The Bible is full of demonstrations of his feelings; no one can say that, because he is God, he did not suffer seeing his Son suffer for all of us. He gave his only Son out of love for the world. How do we understand the biblical verse? for the sake of every human being, imperfect, sinful or not, Jewish or not, obedient and disobedient, absolutely, for all of us.

As true Christians, obeying for love implies fulfilling the will of God for love of Him, Jesus, the Holy Spirit and, above all, our neighbor.

In this regard, the apostle John in his first letter mentioned: We know that we love the children of God if we love God and obey his commandments. Loving God means obeying his commandments, and his commandments are not a difficult burden to bear.

Almost everything we do in the world is for others. Our jobs satisfy the needs of others, few things are for us.

Obedience to Jesus Christ proves our love. Immersed in a spiritual war for the struggle of souls, obedience must reach the highest level; out of fear of the Lord, out of convenience and out of love. Out of fear of the Lord, we might be able to sacrifice our son; out of convenience we decided to belong and help in the family of God; Only in obedience out of love will we be able to give our lives for others, and I don't mean to receive a shot for another (although you can also), I mean to offer the rest of our lives for service to others.

In hell, the servant of God received revelation about the holy army that Jesus is preparing. It's an army of all ages, men, women, children, young people, and all saints, anointed to boldly preach the true gospel. People anointed to lay their hands on the sick and heal them in the name of Jesus, anointed people to call sinners to repentance.

Simple human beings, because many nobles have not answered my call —said Jesus.

Diverse people, who, perhaps, in the past were misunderstood or mistreated, abused or rejected. To them, God will bless, granting them boldness in holiness and in Spirit. With the elect the prophecies will be fulfilled and His will, will be done.

To the servant of God, Jesus told her:

—I will walk in them, I will speak in them and I will work in them because they have turned to me with all my heart, soul, mind and strength. They will awaken many to my justice and purity of spirit. I will soon begin to move among them, to choose those I wish for my army. I will look for them in the nations. Many will be surprised by those I have chosen. They will move over the whole earth and will do great deeds for the sake of my name.

I believe it, for two reasons. The first, these statements have biblical support. The second, in my spirit I received the instruction to believe him. That army of God needs to be pure; Christians cannot taint the marriage bed, or our body, where the Holy Spirit dwells. The sins of the body lead to sins of the Spirit.

God made man for woman and woman for man. He decreed that they be united in holy matrimony. Christian families who have sex without the blessing of marriage, need to marry, otherwise are in fornication. Satan uses any valid argument to harm us, fornication is one of them. The blessing of God closes that gap.

From hell, the servant of God saw how all kinds of evil were thrown on the earth.

However, Jesus told him:

—Daughter, in my name the evil has to flee. Put on the full armor of God so that you can stand firm on bad days, and having done everything, stand firm.

Likewise, she saw how, on earth, when people prayed and believed God, the forces of evil were destroyed. Where there is unbelief, the powers of evil advance. We have worship. If the praises of the people of God rise from the earth, the forces of evil withdraw from the place.

God offers us the spiritual tools to face the battles; it depends on us, to use them. In the armor of God, we have his word, which is a sword against Satan and his allies.

Remember, when Jesus Christ was tempted in the desert, He always defeated Satan with the word of God. As an army of God, we have that spiritual weapon. The spiritual is only overcome in the spiritual. «At the precise moment, I heard you. On the day of salvation I helped you ». Indeed, the "precise moment" is now. Today is the day of salvation —says

God in his word, to that we must hold on. We need to be strong in Jesus Christ and his power.

In this regard, the apostle Paul culminated his letter to the church of Ephesus with the following recommendation: —Be strong in the Lord and in his great power. Put on the full armor of God to be able to stand firm against all the strategies of the devil; for we do not fight against flesh and blood enemies, but against evil rulers and authorities of the invisible world, against powerful forces of this dark world and against evil spirits of the heavenly places. Therefore, put on all the pieces of God's armor to be able to resist the enemy in the time of evil. Thus, after the battle, they will still stand, firm. Defend your position, putting on the belt of truth and the breastplate of God's justice. Put on footwear the peace that comes from the Good News in order to be fully prepared. On top of all that, raise the shield of faith to stop the devil's burning arrows. Put salvation as a helmet and take the sword of the Spirit, which is the word of God. Pray in the Spirit at all times and on all occasions. Stay alert and be persistent in your prayers for believers everywhere.

Many churches avoid preaching those messages, they aren't popular, and they don't want to listen to them. We must invite to face the battle for the struggle of souls. The preaching of prosperity, replaced spiritual warfare. We gain nothing by being prosperous, rich, millionaires, yes, spiritually, we are dead.

In hell, Jesus told that servant of God, like, one of those preachers who were suffering, He commanded him to repent for all the people who led wrong and taught him false doctrines. He asked her to confess his sin publicly. That preacher did not want to. Thus, he arrived at his eternal destiny.

The trips of that servant to hell happened in 1976. In visions, she observed Christians who were born and the angels were placed over them to protect them from evil. He looked at the God of armies fighting their battles, winning victories for those Christians. He saw those babies grow and harvest the fields of the Lord, they did their work with happy hearts, they loved God, and they trusted in Him, they served Jesus. He observed angels and the word of God united, destroying the evil on earth. Finally, he saw peace on this planet.

In my case, I was born in 1977; maybe I am one of those children she saw. Although I received Jesus Christ at my thirty-sixth birthday, one day, I saw how I was protected by God all my life.

If you are a Christian and you are reading these lines, remember, God protected you from birth. If you have abused the grace to live in sin and you have not repented then you are on time, ensure your salvation. You can die at any time, don't trust yourself, you need to keep your accounts up to date with Him.

If you are not a Christian yet Open your heart and loudly, whether alone or accompanied, have this prayer:

"Lord JESUS, today I open my heart to receive you, I recognize that I have disobeyed you, I have lived away from you and I repent, I ask your forgiveness for all my sins. I give myself to you; I give you my anxieties, problems, needs, fears, resentments and plans. I recognize you as my only and sufficient Savior. Please write my name in the book of life, fulfill your purpose in me, and teach me the way, the truth and the life that you are. Your kingdom come to me. Amen".

Remember that God didn't send his Son into the world to condemn the world, but to save it through him. Jesus Christ wants to save you from hell.

If you still don't have an attitude of spiritual militancy, seek the will of God in prayer and ask him: Lord Jesus, what is my role in your army? In his own way, in the right way, at the precise moment, He will answer you.

Help God in this lost society, far from his will. Jesus Christ doesn't want anyone to go to hell. He made us for his eternal communion.

We are his creation and he loves us, God wants to do great things with us.

When Jesus sought me, I obeyed his call out of love for my son, not even for my own sake, I couldn't afford to let my child die. Some father could be shot for saving his son that was not my case, for love of my son I gave my life to serve God until my death, maybe 80 years more. To live, we need spirit, soul and body.

In my performance as a servant of Jesus, God commands me to be in excellent physical condition. It doesn't serve just to take care of the spirit. Christians who neglect their body, believing themselves to be spiritual, are in sin. God commands to take care of the temple of the Holy Spirit. We must love God, ourselves (health), and our neighbor. In my case, I don't know if inherited, or in the sins of my own lust, I grabbed a spirit of heartbreak, difficult to uproot. It cost me to realize the dominance of that evil spirit over my life. With fasting, prayer and the power of the Holy Spirit, I managed to overcome it. Now, I can love.

Now, every night before I sleep, I give my heart control to God, to cleanse me. As a small child I ask him to sleep in his chest, his sanctity and purity is the only thing that can cleanse my spirit. Some dreams are liberating, asleep I experience circumstances that awake I would face in another way, and there I see the true reactions that come from my heart. With the Bible, I understood why God communicated with me in dreams. I read, some affirmations, in which, Job said:

—Well, God speaks again and again, even if people do not recognize it. It speaks in dreams, in night visions, when deep sleep falls on people while they are lying down. Whispers to their ears and terrorizes them with warnings. He causes them to turn away from their evil deeds; do not let them fall into pride. He protects them from the grave, from crossing the river of death.

Dreams are a valid alternative for God. He can communicate with us, like this. In my case, not all dreams come from God. I seek relief in his dreams, the rest I forget.

In dreams, I saw the evolution of my feelings for my wife. God, little by little, cleaned my heart. At first, asleep, I unleashed my anger against her; there was rector in my heart. In my mind, I thought, everything was fine, but dreams revealed the opposite. In dreams, I began to endure it, then to treat her with love, until, finally, to tell her that I loved her.

In reconciliation with my wife, to obey God out of love, it's not enough only to love God, Jesus Christ, the Holy Spirit, my son; it's necessary to love my wife. Before Jesus, that is an important part of: being prepared to receive her.

My wife is a chosen one of God. She has a purpose for Jesus Christ. It was my mistakes that opened the spiritual breaches, which Satan used to take possession of my marriage.

In one of the trips to hell, the servant of God saw the quarter of trophies of Satan. There, he accumulates what he manages to take away from the children of God, either by preventing them from receiving him or by taking advantage of mistakes. In her visit to heaven, the servant of God saw rooms, barns, with blessings stored for the people of God. Each son or daughter of God has his own barn. There, we have money, goods, many things; even from materials to body parts.

How can Satan avoid receiving that?

When God promises us something, in general, we don't receive it immediately, we must always believe it. Satan aims to delay the blessing, so that, in our lack of persistence, we ourselves will lose it. If we stop believing in the miracle, even the day before, hours before, we can stop receiving it. That is why many miracles take time or never come. According to the Bible, analyzing verses from the book of Genesis, twenty-five years passed from the promise, until the day when Isaac, the son of Abraham, was born. Depending on the influence in the struggle for the souls, our miracles can, take more time if they will influence much, and less time if they will influence little. After all, Satan cares to steal, kill and destroy every human being. If the blessing God for someone doesn't represent problems in his evil, then, he doesn't oppose much. On the contrary, if the blessing will influence the salvation of souls, it will do everything possible to delay it, it will fight to avoid it.

Satan cannot take away miracles or promises, we lose them by ourselves when we don't believe or don't persist in the faith until we receive them. As a Satan trophy, I saw my wife in a dream. In that case, she was not something that Satan managed to avoid, I managed to marry her. My wife was booty of Satan because he took advantage of my mistakes, including the main one, my adultery. Without Jesus in me, I hated my wife. That sin of the flesh, passed to my heart.

That happens in millions of families in the world. Derailed children, parents, mothers outside the will of God, husbands, unconverted wives, spiritual warfare is something real that few recognize.

Thanks to the mercy of God, He has decided to reveal many mysteries to us, his children. As we grow spiritually, we receive spiritual breast milk, then solid spiritual food. That is, first, we obtain basic revelation of the word of God, before we understand the advance.

When I was a child, I spoke thought and reasoned like a child; but when I grew up, I left behind things as a child. Now we see everything imperfectly, like disconcerting reflections, but then we will see everything with perfect clarity. Everything I know now is partial and incomplete, but then I will know everything completely, just as God already knows me completely — said the Apostle Paul, in this regard, in his first letter to the Corinthians.

Now, that my wife was booty of Satan didn't indicate the impossibility of Jesus Christ to take it from her. Remember the gospel of Mark, as Jesus said:

— Who has enough power to enter the house of a strong man like Satan and plunder his property? Well, only someone even stronger, someone who could tie him up and then ransack his house.

That man, even stronger, is Jesus Christ.

It was Jesus who freed my wife from Satan. Although the reconciliation has not happened, and has not even returned to live in this city, our family has already been reconciled in the spiritual world. God showed it to me, I believe it, and I still wait. He knows when I will be ready to receive it. My wife, my son, his daughter and a girl who is still to be born, all of us, were chosen by God to fulfill a purpose for Jesus. We must fulfill it for love.

So he will speak all the languages of the world and of the angels but he will not love others, I would just be a loud metal or a cymbal that resonates. If I had the gift of prophecy and understood the entire secret plans of God and had all the knowledge, and if I had a faith that would make me capable of moving mountains, but not loving others, I would be nothing. If I gave everything I have to the poor and even sacrificed my body, I could boast of that; but if he did not love others, he would have achieved nothing —

said the apostle Paul in his first letter to the Corinthians.

Loving God, and loving our neighbor, is the first commandments, the most important ones, of which lies the success of our service to Jesus Christ. Without love we are nothing, the Apostle Paul explained it. We must focus on obeying God for fear of the Lord (avoiding hell), also, obeying God out of convenience (believing the full reward in heaven) and obeying God out of love (protecting the undeserved gift, our salvation, until the end).

Beyond warnings

My family and I need to fill our hearts with the love of God; in love we will fulfill the individual and collective purpose for which he chose us. The rest of our lives, we must serve Jesus Christ. We depend on loving others, because without love for our neighbor, we can never give our lives for them, let alone persevere until the end.

I wrote this book as a special warning for millions of people, whom, Satan, has deceived within Christian congregations.

Those of us who have been redeemed and chosen by Jesus Christ have the responsibility to fulfill the will of God on earth. We, the believers of this generation, have been called to lead spiritual warfare against the evil one and his allies. The evil one knows it. His main battle is to deceive us to get one, several or all the members of Christian families away from Jesus.

In this work, I emphasized the preaching of grace without repentance. I highlighted that, because it's the main deception within the current church. It's not the only one. The Pastors deceived by Satan, are preaching popular messages. From the pulpits, many people are being guided not to follow the true gospel with the whole word of God.

Promises without conditions; freedom of man without sovereignty of God: Power without character, Restoration without discipline, Self-esteem without breaking, Responsibility without spontaneity, Faith without works, Anointing without excellence, Justification without sanctification, Free will without Jesus' Lordship. Those half-truths come out of pulpits where the full gospel is not preached, the word of God balanced.

Repentance reveals the will of God while grace gives us the equipment to be forgiven by Him. Divine promises have conditions, but the "friendly" gospel makes them obvious. That is why many Christians don't reach them.

The freedom of the human being to make his own decisions doesn't condition God to do what He has not promised to do. The sovereignty of Jesus Christ never nullifies our freedom of selection. Jesus never compels us to anything, we choose ourselves. We are free to go to hell, if we want.

Teaching power to Christians, without orienting ourselves in the formation of character, is dangerous. That can destroy anyone. Samson killed himself with his own unction, without the proper character, yielded to Delilah.

The restoration reveals God as Father, merciful. Discipline reveals God to us, as Just. Both aspects are indispensable.

Anointing doesn't replace excellence; they complement each other to fulfill our responsibilities. To attribute everything bad to Satan, without taking into account the lust (desires not pleasing to God) of our flesh leads us to attack the problem in a wrong way. The demons are cast out; the desires of the flesh are crucified.

Self-esteem, to believe that everything we can in Christ that strengthens us, is complemented, with the breaking of the spirit to do the will of God. Faith without works is dead, works don't save us, works follow faith; when faith doesn't produce works then it's not true faith. Responsibility guides us to fulfill the will of God, but, the Spirit of God can change our plans whenever we want. We need to be open to the spontaneity of the Holy Spirit.

We cannot use justification to deny sanctification. With justification, God decrees us justified before Him, sanctification is obedience to His word. We are righteous by the blood of Jesus Christ but holy by our obedience to the word of God, to the Holy Spirit and to the power of the blood of Jesus Christ. We are righteous by grace, not by works. Without holiness no one will see the Lord. Like every human being, we Christians have free will but Jesus Christ is the Lord of our freedom. Without the lordship of Jesus, we are mistaken, we deceive ourselves, and we believe we are free to fulfill the desires of the flesh and / or yield to the temptations of Satan. We all need the Holy Spirit.

The Holy Spirit can preach the same theme, in different churches, in simultaneous periods. God has general strategies for the church of Jesus and his pastors can agree on such issues. However, we must take care of the fashionable issues; popular preaching, without divine revelation.

For example, the preaching of poverty predominated as a teaching within the churches. Now, preaching the gospel of prosperity prevails, without a healthy balance. The preaching of the gospel of the kingdom teaches us to give and to receive. Jesus Christ, out of love for us, became poor, so that through his poverty, he could make us rich. Prosperity in the people of God is necessary, but without equilibrium, money can become our master, when money should be our servant.

The struggle for souls needs various resources, including financial ones. Servants of God also need money resources to cover our personal and family needs, in addition to helping in the expansion of God's kingdom on earth. The growth of the influence of Jesus, in different sectors of society; it needs resources, money. He wants servants, millionaires, for his work; Millionaires with character, servants, faithful in small quantities, before administering the big ones. Throughout the Bible, there are no cases of people in hell being poor; if there are cases of the people of God, servants, who mismanaged their wealth and ended up in outer darkness.

Remember the parable of the three servants, Jesus taught clearly about the use of money, He said: —A man who had to undertake a long journey gathered his servants and entrusted his money to them while he was absent. He divided it in proportion to the capacities of each one. To the first one he gave five bags of silver; to the second one, two bags of silver; and the last one, a single bag of silver. Then he went on travel. The servant who received the five bags of silver began to invest the money and won five more. The one with the two silver bags also went to work and won two more. But the servant who received a single bag of silver dug a hole in the ground and there hid the money of his master. After a long time, the master returned from his trip and called them to give an account of how they had used their money. The servant to whom he had entrusted the five bags of silver presented he with five more and said: "Master, you gave me five bags of silver to invest, and I have won five more." The master filled him with praise. "Well done, my good faithful servant. You have been faithful in administering this small amount, so now I will give you many more responsibilities. Come celebrate with me! "The servant who had received the two bags of silver presented himself and said: "Master, you gave me two bags of silver to invest, and I won two more." The master said: "Well done, my good faithful servant. You have been faithful in administering this small amount, so now I will give you many more responsibilities. Come celebrate with me! "

Both were called good faithful servants.

However, regarding the third, Jesus taught:

—Finally the servant who had only one bag of silver presented him and said: "Master, I knew that you were a severe man, that you harvest what you did not sow and pick up the crops that you did not cultivate. I was afraid of losing your money, so I hid it on earth. Look, here's your money back. "But the master replied: "Wicked and lazy servant! If you knew that I reaped what I did not sow and I collected what I did not cultivate, why did not you deposit my money in the bank? At least I could have gotten some interest from him. "Then he ordered: "Take the money from this servant and give it to the one who has the ten bags of silver. Those who make good use of what is given to them will be given even more and will have abundance; but those who do nothing will be taken away even what little they have. Now, throw this useless servant into the darkness outside, where there will be weeping and gnashing of teeth. "

As we read, someone who serves God, a servant, whether man or woman, if mismanaged the resources of Jesus Christ can be thrown into the dark outside, where there is crying and gnashing of teeth. His eternal destiny can be suffering in hell.

The preaching of the gospel of prosperity without proper balance omits those teachings. Wealth, without obedience to God, can be a curse. Those messages are not popular, they are necessary.

It's essential to understand that every army has its hierarchical organization. God gives the strategies, Jesus Christ establishes the tactics and we are responsible for the operations. Our Chief is Jesus; He is the intermediary before God, the Great Chief.

To believe that we do God's will, without taking Jesus Christ into account, is a deception. In my case, when asking about the gun in my head, I heard: only God the Father is reached through me —Jesus told me.

As God the Father is the one who directs the strategies in spiritual warfare, He selects our area of influence. Which city? Municipality? What to do? That is determined by God, we know it through Jesus Christ, through the Holy Spirit. Facing the spiritual war, obeying our criteria, in the city where we think is better, sector where we like, doing it our way, brings losses, consequences in us and in God's people.

In my case, I am established in Valencia, a city in Venezuela. I was chosen to teach a lifestyle pleasing to God, through books, based on real events. My main sector to carry the message of Jesus is sport. I must do it running to lift a brand of sportswear. That is my main contribution in the battle for the struggle of souls, but it's not the only one. When I gave my life to Christ, I didn't ask: what? With whom? Nor how much I was going to pay. He uses me in what he wants, moves me where he wants.

If he will act under my own will, without receiving the instructions of Jesus Christ, he would live in Merida, my hometown. I would share the message of Jesus in the university sector, and I would do so by giving lectures to the students. That would offer me temporary joy, and then I would feel, again, empty. It happens to me in sports. I like to swim, when I leave the pool I feel empty. I don't like running, when competing, even when training, I feel fullness difficult to explain.

To move in my will, outside of God's plans would be mortal. I emphasize, not serious. I reiterate, mortal. If we get out of the will of Jesus Christ we can lose the divine protection that God assigns us, He can remove, from us, his protective angels. Without the protecting angels of God, without Jesus Christ in me and without the Angel of Jehovah of Hosts camping beside me, I am an easy prey for Satan. That privilege of protection, I have proven it, many times. That is not a privilege, just for me. Every person who belongs to the army of the living God because, he militates in the struggle for the salvation of souls, always has privileges of heavenly protection.

On the contrary, those who don't seek direction from Jesus and face the battle with their own strategy don't advance and even die in the war. To enter into spiritual warfare without being guided by God, without Jesus, without obeying the Holy Spirit, is a severe mistake. The protection to survive on earth, and in spiritual warfare, depends on abiding by the will of God in all his strategies of expansion of His kingdom.

My direct family is also assigned by God to the same city, and sector, although they vary in how to do it, according to their particular gifts. In my case, I have to run, my son to play soccer. My wife must manage the clothing brand.

Each one of us must fulfill his personal purpose within a family purpose. When the time comes, we will have to give an account to Jesus Christ individually, to fulfill, or not, his call.

In a dream, I saw a group of people wearing t—shirts of the sportswear brand, we were wearing them, we were climbing stairs, I don't know where. My wife, I didn't have those clothes. Suddenly, she was thrown out, into a place of darkness. When I woke up, I searched for the revelation. At that time, I understood that the clothing brand was a major part of her purpose for God through Jesus.

I need to clarify, so as not to leave gaps of misinterpretation. No clothes offer salvation, it can serve to lead a nice lifestyle before God, yes, because with something we have to dress.

Salvation depends on Jesus, to believe in our hearts that God raised him from the dead, and confess him as our only Lord and Savior.

For our sake, we need to know Jesus as Lord, Pastor, Provider, Healer, Brother, Savior, Redeemer, live for Him, obey Him every day, in everything. Love him always. Fulfill your call.

Among the deceptions of Satan, is to guide us to think that we can be saved without fulfilling our call. If we don't fulfill our call it's because we never obeyed, we really knew Jesus. If we didn't know Jesus, we didn't reach God the Father.

We can lose our salvation by not fulfilling the call, that purpose for which God created us.

Certainly, all sin can be forgiven, except for the blasphemy of the Holy Spirit. But, if someone is not fulfilling his purpose, he needs to repent, take advantage of the grace and ask God for forgiveness so that he can immediately surrender to Jesus and be used for the rest of his days in the struggle for souls.

That is our great commission, Jesus said:

—I have been given all authority in heaven and on earth. Therefore, go and make disciples of all nations, baptizing them in the name of the Father and of the Son and of the Holy Spirit. Teach the new disciples to obey all the commands I have given them. And be assured of this: I am with you always, until the end of time.

By making new disciples, we liberate souls from the domain of Satan and give them to God. Therefore, in the Gospel of Mark, we read, Jesus said:

—Go around the world and preach the Good News to everyone. He who believes and is baptized will be saved but he who refuses to believe will be condemned.

What city? Municipality? With what gifts?

That only God, Jesus Christ and Holy Spirit knows. When reading these lines, someone may ask: how can I know what my purpose is? if I didn't hear the voice of God, neither Jesus, nor Holy Spirit.

If you have that doubt, open your heart and ask sincerely to Jesus Christ to reveal his purpose. God is interested in revealing His plan to you, He requires true soldiers within His army. Every Christian has the duty to preach the gospel because, as Jesus commanded it, before going to heaven.

In my case, one afternoon someone told me:

—Jesus is by your side, he wants you to know, He saved your life because you have a purpose to fulfill.

When I received that message I worked in an international company. Months went by until I knew what my purpose was, my task for God.

From one day to the next, I felt, in me, a deep conviction to leave the company. God's plan for me, in that organization, had already been fulfilled.

When I decided to resign, Jesus Christ helped me. One night, I sensed that the next morning they would ask me to resign. While we were having dinner, I asked a girlfriend, who was an accountant, to do the math for me. How much money did I need to live on my own for three years, without detracting from my quality of life?

She took her calculator and showed me a set.

If tomorrow they offer me a Bolivar (Venezuelan currency) more than that amount, I sign my resignation —I said, seeing the figure.

That's how it went. Early on, when I arrived at my office, the director of the company called me and asked me to resign. Due to the economic crisis in Venezuela, the organization decided to suspend its investment projects. My main responsibility was to direct those projects, and, without foreign investment, my position was unnecessary. When I heard the number for my resignation, I smiled and accepted. The amount exceeded my expectation.

For the date, six months had passed since I received the revelation of Jesus, calling me to fulfill a purpose. I had no idea what I should do for Him. When I stopped working I felt I had to take a vacation time, I relaxed and started to travel.

Suddenly, on one of those trips, my father carried my son on his shoulders, without suspecting anything; I took a picture of them. When I saw the image, I felt in my heart: "I will write a book, this will be the cover".

When I returned to my home, I sat for seven days and wrote my testimony, including reflections from important books in my life. At that time, I didn't include the Bible; I didn't feel able to use it.

That, my first book, I wrote without worrying about spelling or grammar, I just sat down and plastered my thoughts of thanks to God.

I wrote it as a gift to God.

I can compare it to a small child, who draws a picture and gives it to his father. Perhaps for another person they are only stripes, for the father it can be art. I believe that my words in that book went directly to the heart of God, because, then, he called me, he formed me and he chose me as a writer for Jesus Christ. In spite of living in Valencia, playing in sports and running, exalting the name of Jesus, my main purpose is to teach a pleasant way of life before God. For that, I try to do everything in my power and use his word revealed in the old and New Testament. I pass through tests, I accumulate experiences, I live my testimonies, to demonstrate, with real facts, how, applying the teachings of Jesus, and we can live to please God. Even in our days, 21st century, before a society far from our Almighty Creator.

Forty months passed, from listening that I had a purpose for Jesus, to knowing the main plans of God for me. The time and manner of them to reveal their plan, may be different. God is original; Jesus can guide you as He wants.

Dear reader, whether you are male or female, in this spiritual war of our times, we need to fulfill all the purpose for which God chose us. To die before fulfilling it, means to leave it halved. Jesus wants Christians to take care of their health, exercise, eat healthy, die of healthy old age.

In spiritual warfare we need to protect the spirit, soul and body. Current congregations focus on the spirit and soul, without caring for the body. They prefer to trust miracles of healing, when many of those diseases could have prevented them. Satan takes advantage of this; every Christian who neglects his health dies before his time.

Any disobedience to the word of God is Satan's argument to kill, steal or destroy Christians. Neglecting the body, our temple of the Holy Spirit is a grave sin.

The only sinner who has no forgiveness is blasphemy against the Holy Spirit. Blasphemy against Jesus could be forgiven by God. Our Holy Spirit is the spoiled child of them, if we are admonished to sadden him, when more to neglect his temple, the body, dwelling in us.

In general, physical health through carelessness in not exercising or eating healthy is the main weak point, visible, within the current congregations. If God doesn't find fully obedient servants within the churches, he will seek them out.

The athletes are a good alternative in the revival that God has planned in the coming years. They know how to obey, they have discipline, and they take care of themselves; releasing them from sins, filling them with love, baptizing them in the Holy Spirit, redeeming them, saving them, teaching them to care for their salvation. Directed by Jesus Christ, they will be powerful warriors.

Spiritual warfare merits absolute obedience to God. For example, let's think about the World War II. Imagine each soldier doing what he liked best. Undoubtedly, most would not even have survived several days. Without obeying orders, every soldier would have failed; without fighting as a team no territory would have been conquered, nobody is enough to take possession of a region.

As Christians we need to stop thinking about fighting or defending my home without thinking about the expansion of the kingdom of God. Jesus Christ needs us. Human beings are the ones who bring the divine blessing to the earth. If our Heavenly Father decided to defeat Satan with humans, then, we must face responsibility as a family, struggle to reach all our brothers of faith in Jesus Christ.

Those of us who belong to the family, know that someone fought for us in prayer. This war needs everyone, in their responsibility of combat, apostles, pastors, evangelists, prophets, teachers, leaders, disciples, all of us useful and necessary in the unification of the body of Christ, that is, the unification of the church. Congregations need mature Christians, producers and not just consumers of the Word of God. To assemble is part of our spiritual life, it's not everything. Studying the Bible, praying, fasting, other things, are necessary in a style of life pleasing to God. To please Jesus Christ, in all areas of our life, is the best life insurance we can have.

Intimacy with Jesus Christ is not achieved only by going to church; it's indispensable 'to lead a pleasant life before God. There are places where the Holy Spirit doesn't have to be, conversations that sadden him. From the daily work of each Christian depends his relationship with God the Father, God the Son and God the Holy Spirit. The intimacy with each one of them is indispensable. We are a family of four or more people; the three of them, me and the rest of mine. Everything except man or woman needs to take care of the unearned gift of salvation because, if you don't take care of it, you may end up suffering in hell; Even if they have followed and served Jesus for a time. If they turn away from God, they don't return, they don't repent in time, they will suffer eternally, and when, dead, they want to appeal to grace, they could respond to him: "you abused the grace of the Lord". Brother or sister who read these lines, don't trust you. If you sin, repent, if you sinned again, repent again, ask for forgiveness as many times as necessary, don't abuse grace; I insist. it's preferable that you repent. Also, fulfill your eternal purpose. In dreams I was warned, we must fulfill our purpose, we can never escape from fulfilling it because we can lose salvation.

I hope this book serve as a warning to myself and to each person to whom Jesus decided to reveal this truth: Satan yearns for our soul; we need to guard our salvation until the last breath on earth. Salvation can be lost.

I love you, with all my heart! Luis Dávila.

To God the Father, our Heavenly Father.

The Big Boss.

—

To God the Son, Jesus, our Savior.

The Boss.

—

To God the Holy Spirit, our guide.

The faithful friend.

Dear reader, Jesus wants to come into your heart. I invite you to greet doing, loudly, this sentence that changed my life: —Lord God, I confess that I am a sinner. I confess that I need your Son Jesus. Please forgive me in His name. Lord Jesus, I believe you died for me and that you are alive and listening me now. I now turn from my sins and welcome you into my heart. Come and take control of my life. Make me kind of person you want me to be. Now, fill me with your Holy Spirit, who will show me how to live for you and acknowledge you before men as my Savior and my Lord. In Jesus´ name, Amen

World Ministry of Teaching

100% JESUS

www.100JESUS.org

www.amazon.com/author/luisdavila

Printed in Great Britain
by Amazon